EXILES AND ÉMIGRÉS

By the same author

★

SHAKESPEARE AND SOCIETY

EXILES
AND ÉMIGRÉS

Studies in Modern Literature

By

TERRY EAGLETON

SCHOCKEN BOOKS · NEW YORK

FOR
ROSEMARY

Published in U.S.A. in 1970
by Schocken Books Inc.
67 Park Avenue, New York, N.Y. 10016

© Terry Eagleton 1970

Second Printing, 1972

Library of Congress Catalog Card No. 70–130207

Manufactured in the United States of America

CONTENTS

ACKNOWLEDGEMENTS

The quotations from the poetry of W. H. Auden, from *Collected Shorter Poems 1927-1957* and *1930-1944* are protected by copyright and have been reprinted by permission of the author, Faber & Faber Ltd., London, and Random House, Inc., New York. Thanks are also due to the copyright owners and publishers of the following works for permission to quote from them in this volume: Joseph Conrad *Under Western Eyes*: the Trustees of the Joseph Conrad Estate and J. M. Dent & Sons Ltd.; T. S. Eliot *Collected Poems 1909-1962*: Faber & Faber Ltd., London, and Harcourt, Brace Jovanovich Inc., New York. *Copyright* 1936 by Harcourt, Brace Jovanovich Inc. and *Copyright* 1963, 1964, by T. S. Eliot; George Orwell *Burmese Days, Coming Up For Air, A Clergyman's Daughter, Keep the Aspidistra Flying, The Road to Wigan Pier*: Miss Sonia Brownell, Secker & Warburg Ltd., London, and Harcourt, Brace Jovanovich Inc., New York; Evelyn Waugh *Decline & Fall, Vile Bodies, A Handful of Dust* and *Brideshead Revisited*: A. D. Peters & Co., London, and Little, Brown and Co., New York. *Copyright* 1944, 1945 by Evelyn Waugh; H. G. Wells *The History of Mr. Polly*: The Executors of H. G. Wells; Virginia Woolf *Mrs Dalloway*: Quentin Bell, Angelica Garnett and The Hogarth Press Ltd., London, and Harcourt, Brace Jovanovich Inc., New York. *Copyright* 1925 by Virginia Woolf; *Copyright* 1953 by Leonard Woolf; *The Collected Poems of W. B. Yeats*: M. B. Yeats and Macmillan & Co., London, and The Macmillan Company, New York. *Copyright* 1933 by The Macmillan Company, renewed 1961 by Bertha Georgie Yeats, for 'Blood and the Moon' and 'Coole Park and Ballylee, 1931'; and *Copyright* 1924 by The Macmillan Company, renewed 1962 by Bertha Georgie Yeats, for 'Meditations in Time of Civil War' and 'Easter, 1916'.

INTRODUCTION

Exiles and Émigrés

IF it is agreed that the seven most significant writers of twentieth-century English literature have been a Pole, three Americans, two Irishmen and an Englishman, then it might also be agreed that the paradox is odd enough to warrant analysis. With the exception of D. H. Lawrence, the heights of modern English literature have been dominated by foreigners and émigrés: Conrad, James, Eliot, Pound, Yeats, Joyce. The aim of this Introduction will not be to attempt any total explanation of this complex phenomenon, but to suggest, in an inevitably curtailed and schematic form, a perspective within which it can be examined and understood. The aim of this whole study, similarly, will not be to provide an exhaustive or systematic account of the theme of expatriatism in modern literature, but rather to offer a series of critical explorations, at once autonomous and interrelated, which centre around a number of general problems raised by the 'émigré' theme.[1]

If the creative literature of a society is dominated over a specific period by foreigners and expatriates, then it is reasonable to assume that this fact is as revealing of the nature of that society as it is of the writers who approached it from a foreign viewpoint. The contention of this Introduction, to be developed in the chapters that follow, is that the unchallenged sway of non-English poets and novelists in contemporary English literature points to certain central flaws and impoverishments in conventional English culture itself. That culture was unable, of its

---

[1] This theme, and its significance for the structure of twentieth-century English culture, has been given broader treatment in Perry Anderson's *Components of the National Culture* (*New Left Review* No. 50, July–August 1968): an article to which, despite some difference of conclusion in the specific field of literature, I am generally indebted.

own impetus, to produce great literary art: the outstanding art which it achieved has been, on the whole, the product of the exile and the alien. It is this curious fact which needs to be explored and understood.

If we compare the great literary achievements of nineteenth-century Romanticism or realism with the English literary creations of our own century, a striking and significant contrast becomes immediately evident. It is part of the genius of poets like Blake and Wordsworth, or novelists like Dickens and George Eliot, that they are able to fuse the profoundest inwardness with the specific life of their own times with a capacity to generalise that life into the form of a complete vision. In the best work of those writers, the shape and structure of an entire culture can be elicited, by an alert sensitivity to the general forces and significant movements of their societies, from the focused detail of local and concrete experience. The Romantic poet or the great realist novelist writes out of a relationship of intricately detailed intimacy with his society; yet he is also able to grasp that society as a totality, in a way which one might have expected to be genuinely available only to an outsider free of its most immediate pressures. It is integral to the imaginative achievements of Blake, Wordsworth, Dickens and Eliot that they can 'totalise' and 'transcend' those pressures without damage to the quickness and specificity of their feel for concrete life.[1] At the high point of their developments, both realism and Romanticism were able to discover a point of operative distance from the partial interests and allegiances of their own cultures: a point of balance at which inwardness could combine with an essential externality to produce major art.

It would, of course, be false to interpret the attainment of

[1] Since the terms 'totalisation' and 'transcendence' will occur fairly frequently throughout this study, it is as well to comment briefly upon them here. By 'totalisation' I mean, not a statically conceived whole, but the act of grasping the elements of a culture in their living and changing inter-relations. By 'transcendence' I mean, not a spiritual movement beyond history and culture, but the historical action of projecting oneself beyond the limits and pressure of a particular settlement into a wider perspective.

this point of balance as a kind of nobly omniscient disinterestedness, uncontaminated by particular loyalties and engagements. If it is obvious enough that Blake created major poetry out of a range of specific social beliefs, it should also be obvious that George Eliot created *Felix Holt*, and much besides, out of a range of essentially opposing assumptions. (With this latter point in mind, incidentally, we might do well to examine more closely the supposed superiority to one-sided social attachments of that other nobly disinterested liberal, Matthew Arnold.) The creation of great literature, as the work of Pope and Jane Austen sufficiently illustrates, has no inevitable connection with the surmounting of such concrete social attachments; but it does seem to demand enough interaction between those convictions, and the typifying problems and developments of the whole culture in which they are set, for them to appear as representative rather than as narrowly partisan. In the nineteenth century, that interaction between particular commitments and the structure of a whole society was active and vigorous enough, whether as conflict or as congruency, for great literature to be possible; the argument of this book will be that its virtual disappearance in the twentieth century, along with the point of balance where it belonged, is an impoverishment significantly related to the entry of the émigrés.

There are, evidently enough, numerous viewpoints from which the general development of the twentieth-century English novel may be discussed, but one of the viewpoints which I have selected for this study, and which I believe relates closely to its central topic, is that of social class. It should hardly be necessary to add that this does not seem to me in general either an exclusive, or necessarily the most productive, critical category, and I am, of course, aware of the severe penalties which contemporary criticism has in store for anyone rash enough to venture the suggestion that 'literature' and 'class' can be significantly related. What I am concerned with is not some crude reduction of imaginative literature to a kind of 'class-determinism': that is to say, with the method often, and wrongly, thought to be Marxist. I am concerned to see the ways in which the social attitudes adopted by particular twentieth-century writers shape or limit their power to achieve that sense of interrelation between concrete living and the shape of a complete culture which the greatest nineteenth-century authors displayed. For this purpose, I have isolated two strands in the development of modern English fiction which I have called the 'upper-class' and 'lower middle-class' novel. Neither of these terms is exact, and neither is meant to indicate either the existence of conscious and consolidated traditions, or the assumption that the novels in question cannot be treated in widely different ways. But they point to some broad ranges of attitude within modern fiction, and their function is no more and no less emphatic than that.

In the closing decades of the nineteenth century, a species of Zolaesque naturalism, influenced by the philosophy of Comte and Spencer, took shallow root in England in the writing of Gissing, Moore and others. It was this strain which reached its fullest expression in Edwardian England, in the work of Shaw, Bennett, Wells and their more minor associates. The class-background of these writers is worth noting: Gissing, born in Wakefield, studied at Owen's College, Manchester, and lived in poverty as a private schoolmaster; Shaw, son of a Dublin corn-factor, was educated at the Wesleyan Connexional school and started work with a firm of estate agents; Bennett, son of a Burslem solicitor and educated in Nonconformist Burslem and Newcastle, worked for a while as a journalist; Wells, son of a hardware dealer and educated at a local grammar school, worked for a draper and later for a solicitor. The lower or 'middling' middle-class ethos is obvious: a provincial, clerical, commercial, Nonconformist, grammar-school milieu. The 'upper-class' novel is very different: Forster, born in London, educated in Cambridge; Virginia Woolf, born in London, daughter of Sir Leslie Stephen, privately educated; Evelyn Waugh, son of a publisher, educated at Oxford; L. H. Myers, born in Cambridge, educated at Eton and Trinity, private means: the list could be extended almost indefinitely. The milieu is metropolitan, privileged, public-school.

In the development of the 'lower middle-class' novel, the social context sketched above intersects with the aesthetic and philosophical emphases of naturalism. The lower middle-class world of Gissing, Bennett, Wells and, later, of Orwell registers itself in a drably detailed, grimly unselective reproduction of 'life as it is'—of the seedy realms of routine social existence beneath the 'conventional' upper-class façades. The 'upper-class' novel, by contrast, is remote from this area: it displays an intense but narrow concern for certain highly selective forms of life and value. It is enclosed and élitist, marooned from the world of working relationships and wider social institutions. Its characteristic centres of intellectual interest are ethics, aesthetics, metaphysics; those of the lower middle-class novel are science, politics, social organisation. The typical ideology of the first is Bloomsbury liberalism; the ideology of the second is Fabianism.

Both of these *genres* are to some extent self-consciously hostile to what they see as the dominant cultural orthodoxy. Lower middle-class naturalism saw its own audacious realism as an assault on bourgeois conventionality, a significant exposure of submerged social realities; the upper-class novel stood counter to that conventionality either in its liberalism and aestheticism, or, as with Waugh, in its nostalgic conservatism. The first *genre* reacted, on the whole, against the hypocrisy of orthodox culture; the second, on the whole, against its philistinism. Yet the truth is that both modes of fiction were tied, at crucial points, to the dominant orthodoxy they opposed. Precisely how this is so will be developed in greater detail in this book; but it is perhaps worth commenting here that Fabianism is the kind of 'radical' ideology, and Bloomsbury the kind of liberal culture, which only a conservative society could have produced. The lower middle-class novel was in general *passively* related to its society: it was a symptom of oppression and frustration, but could not itself transcend the direct pressures of that experience to evaluate it as a whole. The upper-class novel, by contrast, was trapped, not within the crippling limits of routine existence, but within a world so partial, rarefied and fragmentary that it could express little more than the relatively untypical living of a rootless, dispossessed sector of the dominant social class. Both modes, as I hope to show in this study, were incapable either of embracing, or transcending, the society to which they represented a critical reaction, and yet with which they shared a common basis of assumptions. The novel, in consequence, was either constrained by the insistent detail of 'realist' experience or cut damagingly adrift from it, clinging to 'civilised' values which were themselves unable to comprehend more than a relatively small area of contemporary civilisation.

In this general context, the achievement of writers like James and Conrad takes on an evident significance. James and Conrad, as émigrés, chose English society from the outside: both, in different ways, were able to survey it from a broader perspective, and so to grasp what it had to offer them as a complete pattern of culture. Both men chose England for reasons closely linked to the whole structure of its social life: its order, its manners, its settled, varied and traditionalist status. Both, as a result, attained a remarkable inwardness with the character of the society; yet they were also able to bring to bear on the culture a range of experience—of America, Europe, Africa, the East—which went beyond its parochial limits, and with which England could be fruitfully compared. It was out of this tension that James and Conrad created their major work; and it was a tension notably absent in the work of their contemporaries.

Between the death of James in 1916 and the death of Conrad in 1924, the highpoint of literary creativity in the twentieth century is reached. In this period fall Eliot's *Prufrock* (1917) and *The Waste Land* (1922), Joyce's *A Portrait of The Artist as a Young Man* (1916), *Ulysses* (1922), and Pound's *Hugh Selwyn Mauberley* (1920). Lawrence's *Sons and Lovers*, published in 1913.

is followed in 1915 by *The Rainbow* and in 1920 by *Women in Love*; with *The Wild Swans at Coole*, Yeats enters in 1919 on his major creative period.

What is the significance of these dates? The answer is obvious: the years of major achievement in English literature this century are the years spanning the First World War: the period when English civilisation itself was called into radical question. It is this which marks the most crucial difference between what might be termed the 'first' and 'second' phases of expatriatism and exile: between James and Conrad, and those who came after them. James and Conrad settled in England in flight from a lack of established order and civilised manners elsewhere: through the varied complex of motives for their emigration, this thread of purpose can be traced as an element of continuity. After this period, however, exhaustion, futility and disintegration strike at the heart of conventional English society; as war looms and social turbulence spreads throughout Europe, that culture is itself seriously threatened. It is this sense of impending or actual collapse which informs the major work of Eliot, Pound, Yeats, Joyce and Lawrence.

Why then should it be that, at the heart of this felt disintegration, the great art of English literature should have been the work of foreigners and émigrés? One, negative reason has already been suggested: the inability of indigenous English writing, caught within its partial and one-sided attachments, to 'totalise' the significant movements of its own culture. That literature responded to the crisis of its society either with an external cynicism, or with a sense of disgusted futility which was itself a symptom, rather than a creative interpretation, of disturbance. In the novels of the 1920s—in Waugh and Huxley in particular—both responses can be seen to co-exist. Eliot, Pound, Yeats, Joyce and Lawrence, on the other hand, had immediate access to alternative cultures and traditions: broader frameworks against which, in a highly creative tension, the erosion of contemporary order could be situated and partially understood. Yeats reaches back to re-create an anti-bourgeois, native Irish lineage, and in doing so achieves a public poise by which the world of 'merchant and clerk' can be placed and judged. Joyce rejected that native lineage and moved to Europe; but he was able to use some of its tools to create an aesthetic and a mythology within which the determining contemporary experience could be grasped. As the inheritor of a Catholic Irish tradition, Joyce rejected its specific contents; yet he remained enduringly indebted to its totalising forms, within which art and religion, history and politics, could still be seen in organic interconnection. When Joyce remarked that his thought was scholastic in everything but the premises, it was this paradox which he had in mind. The true meaning of the commonplace that Joyce remained a Catholic Irishman lies in the tension, the pattern of attraction and repulsion, the *ambivalent* stance towards his culture which informed all of his work. Both Yeats and Joyce reveal a complex relation to their own societies which was not, on the whole, reproduced in England.

Something similar may be said of T. S. Eliot. Eliot once commented that James was a European in a way that no native of Europe could be, and the point applies with equal force to Eliot himself. The American Eliot was able to place and assimilate what he needed of European culture from the vantage-point of an essentially different tradition; like Yeats and Joyce, he occupied an intrinsically complex and ambiguous position within the society out of which he wrote. More than any other author, Eliot provides a kind of bridge between the 'first' and 'second' phases of the phenomenon under discussion. With an unerring instinct for centrality, he came to Europe and experienced, from the centre, the definitive social reality of his time: the undermining of order and tradition. Yet like James and Conrad, Eliot's expatriate attachment to that tradition, as man and artist, was deeply rooted: the order whose decay he recorded was not his original milieu, but it was one in which his values and instincts were profoundly engaged. When social order was partially re-consolidated in Europe, Eliot stayed in England to re-enact the Jamesian experiment, conforming both his art and theory to the new determinants of established English culture.

Lawrence is the only Englishman among these writers, yet there is one simple biographical fact about him which cannot be overlooked: Lawrence was working-class. He came, that is to say, from a milieu which was in certain ways as ambivalently related to the national culture as Dublin, or even New England: a culture which, like those, belonged and yet was excluded, both foreign and familiar. (It is significant that the only major *English* novelist writing at the end of the nineteenth century, when the field was dominated by James and Conrad, was Thomas Hardy, the grammar-school educated son of a Dorset builder. Hardy, like Lawrence, came from a culture in severe tension with English society, a remote and declining sector far removed from the metropolis.) Lawrence's achievement was to bring to bear, on the disintegrating order of his time, the rich values of a working-class experience: to generalise, from this basis, a critique of England which seemed at times as alien as the judgement of a foreigner, yet as intimately acquainted with its real issues as a native.

The great literary achievements of the war years, then, the art which most intimately caught and evaluated the characteristic experience of the age, was made possible by the existence within English society of alien components. Nothing equivalent was produced by the Second World War: native English writers went to Marxism for their totalising framework, yet it was, on the whole, a curiously domesticated Marxism which, as we shall see in the case of Auden, allowed no genuine transcendence of the controlling social feelings and assumptions. The writers of the earlier period, by contrast, had a more fertile relation to their cultures. In one sense, they were able to dramatise the realities of disintegration because of a striking congruency between the structure of feeling of the whole society and their own most immediate responses as literal or social expatriates. In *A Portrait of The Artist*, *The Rainbow* and *The Waste Land*, a deeply personal disorientation is objectified into a total version of contemporary society; and although the offered versions demand critical discrimination (a point to be exemplified later, in a discussion of Eliot's uses of myth), their range and power cannot be denied. Yet what made such controlled evaluation possible for these writers was an awareness that the declining culture they confronted was in no full sense their own. Penetrating the experience of erosion, in each case, is the felt presence of alternative traditions, whether created or received: for Yeats, Irish mythology and the Anglo-Irish heritage; for Lawrence, the memory of a working-class community; for Eliot, the moral and social milieu of New England and a selection of European aesthetic and intellectual traditions; for Joyce, a comprehensive aesthetic wrestled painfully from the established culture. In no case are these alternatives merely points of refuge: they are themselves deeply implicated in the general undermining of civilised order. For Lawrence, that undermining infiltrates the culture he remembers and erodes its strength; for Yeats, the sway of merchant and clerk symbolises the destruction of traditional aristocracy; for Eliot, spiritual and aesthetic values are menaced by a pervasive bourgeois collapse; for Joyce, the loss of a native culture involves personal exile. In each case, great art is produced, not from the simple availability of an alternative, but from the subtle and involuted tensions between the remembered and the real, the potential and the actual, integration and dispossession, exile and involvement.

It is necessary, finally, to re-emphasise that the studies in this book attempt no systematic analysis of the problem of exile and expatriatism in modern English literature. In particular, I am concerned not so much with the work of the 'literal' expatriates but with the 'social' exiles: with the work of Englishmen who reveal most acutely the cultural limitations which, I have argued, are closely related to the problem of the émigré. The focus of this study is English writers, and the attitudes to society which they display; and for this reason I have concentrated on authors like Evelyn Waugh, George Orwell and

Graham Greene rather than on what may seem the more obvious choices of Henry James and Ezra Pound. The book, in other words, does not attempt to argue directly the issues of literal expatriatism, but rather to use these issues as a general framework within which certain ambivalences in English writing between 'domestic' and 'foreign' experience, interior and exterior ways of perceiving the problems of English culture, may be better understood.

CHAPTER I

Joseph Conrad and 'Under Western Eyes'

THE substance of Conrad's *Under Western Eyes* is a violent and passionate episode of Russian revolutionary history, related by a self-avowedly prosaic and restricted narrator: an English teacher of languages, compassionate but conventional, loyally sympathetic in personal relationship but wholly incapable of interpreting the significance of the turbulent events he observes. The relation between the narrator and his subject-matter provides, in a sense, the total structure of the novel; and the point of this chapter will be to examine its meaning.

In an author's note on *Under Western Eyes*, written in 1920, Conrad himself is interestingly reticent about the purpose of this narrative device. It has, he admits, been heavily criticised since the book first appeared, but he will make no attempt at this late point to justify its existence: it is enough to say that the language-teacher proved 'useful' for his artistic purposes. The uses he then specifies, however, seem less than adequate justification for the technique: they simply concern one or two issues of plot-credibility—the need to produce 'the effect of actuality', to create a credible eye-witness, and so on—which seem curiously disproportionate to the insistence with which the device is employed in the novel. There is an awkward problem about the language-teacher's role in *Under Western Eyes* and a clue to it may be found in another of the book's disturbing emphases: its claim to a dispassionately neutral handling of its own subject-matter.

'My greatest anxiety', Conrad writes in his note, 'was in being able to strike and sustain the note of scrupulous impartiality. . . . I had never been called before to a greater effort of detachment: detachment from all passions, prejudices, and even personal memories.' It is evident enough that a major function of the novel's timidly uncomprehending narrator is to maintain this desired impartiality: since he is unable to interpret the experience he records, he can register no reliable critical attitude towards it. He begins his story by disclaiming both imaginative talent and a 'comprehension of the Russian character'; and from that point onwards the record is regularly interrupted with reminders that the events surrounding Razumov and Nathalie Haldin are inscrutable expressions of an alien oriental temperament which no European can hope to judge. The narrator himself has a 'decent', conventionally English mind unequal to the passionate intensities of the 'Russian soul'; he is 'unidentified with any one in this narrative where the aspects of honour and shame are remote from the ideas of the Western world', and takes his stand on 'the ground of a common humanity', responding sympathetically, but from no defined standpoint. We are reminded, with tediously self-conscious emphasis, that 'this is a Russian story for Western ears, which . . . are not attuned to certain tones of cynicism and cruelty, of moral negation, and even of moral distress . . .'.

One source of this drive to neutrality, evident enough in other of Conrad's works besides this one, can be found in a particular philosophical view of truth. In much of Conrad's later work, a sense of the ineffable elusiveness of truth, of the impossibility of grasping the heart of a fragmentary universe, leads to a continual hedging of every definitive statement with ironic reservations and disclaimers, suggestive of the oblique relativism of all judgement and the partial validity of each linguistic mode. To this extent, then, a dispassionate detachment is intrinsically essential, as a proper response to reality itself; but its necessity is underlined in *Under Western Eyes*, where the major political conflict is one between 'senseless tyranny' on the one hand and 'senseless desperation' on the other. 'The ferocity and imbecility of an autocratic rule rejecting all legality and in fact basing itself upon complete moral anarchism', says Conrad in his authorial note, 'provokes the no less imbecile and atrocious answer of a purely Utopian revolutionism encompassing destruction by the first means to hand. . . .' This, essentially, is the political equation which the novel presents, and it cancels itself out into a void. Anarchists and autocrats, as in *The Secret Agent*, are locked interdependently together within the same grotesquely arbitrary game, each destructively abstracted from the sane, orderly reality—'normal, practical, everyday life'—embodied in different ways by Razumov before his betrayal and the kindly English professor. The novel, consequently, is not formally concerned with political conflict, since on this level there is nothing to choose; it is concerned, Conrad says, with the psychology rather than the politics of Russia, with the 'aspect, character and fate' of individuals. The focus, in other words, shifts from the brutal unrealities of a political game to the isolated, suffering individual trapped within its terms: to Razumov, the uncommitted victim.

That, at least, is the novel's official account of itself, in its author's own, slightly cryptic terms; but it is worth inquiring how far the asserted 'scrupulous neutrality' corresponds to what we actually find in the text. We can note, to begin with, that neutrality in the narrator's sense of avoiding evaluative judgements can, of course, be as much a mode of commitment as explicit partiality: by withholding judgement at a crucial point, it can silently endorse a questionable attitude. Aside from that relatively subtle form of deception, however, there are more obvious ways in which the novel's claim to strict neutrality seems less than justified. In the first place there is the treatment of the anarchists themselves: Sophia Antonovna, Peter Ivanovitch, Madame de S——, Necator and the rest. 'Nobody', says Conrad, 'is exhibited as a monster here— neither the simple-minded Tekla nor the wrong-headed Sophia Antonovna. Peter Ivanovitch and Madame de S—— are fair game. They are the apes of a sinister jungle and are treated as their grimaces deserve. As to (Necator), he is the perfect flower of the terroristic wilderness. What troubled me most in dealing with him was not his monstrosity but his banality.' The whole

statement is significantly ambiguous: 'monstrosity' is disowned
in the first sentence only to re-appear as 'apes' in the second and
be implicitly confessed in the last. In fact, the novel's actual
descriptions of the revolutionaries undeniably confirm the
hollowness of this disclaiming of caricature. Madame de S——
has 'the rigour of a corpse galvanised into harsh speech and
glittering stare by the force of murderous hate'; Ivanovitch is
a megalomanic fraud; Necator is portrayed as a gross, sinisterly
squeaking obscenity. The only really admired revolutionaries
are Miss Haldin and Sophia Antonovna, but the first is attractive
for her character rather than her beliefs, and the magnetism of
the second is significantly qualified:

> How un-Russian she looked, thought Razumov. Her mother
> might have been a Jewess or an Armenian or—devil knew what.
> He reflected that a revolutionist is seldom true to the settled
> type. All revolt is the expression of strong individualism—ran
> his thought vaguely. One can tell them a mile off in any society,
> in any surroundings.

Sophia Antonovna's revolutionary energies are abstracted from
their actual social context and individualised to the level of
temperamental qualities which could be active in any situation.
  In none of these cases can there be any question of 'neutrality':
what we have instead is the indulgence of a half-repelled, half-
fascinated loathing of social revolution which, as the mechanically over-emphatic language used to describe Madame de
S—— reveals, has a tone of uncontrolled fantasy and fear. The
truth is that the novel is shot through with two, almost contra-
dictory, political attitudes. On the one hand there is a form of
genuinely sceptical detachment generated by a sense of inevitable stalemate, of the equal absurdities of both anarchy and
autocracy. 'In this world of men', Razumov reflects, 'nothing
can be changed—neither happiness nor misery. They can only
be displaced at a cost of corrupted consciences and broken
lives—a futile game for arrogant philosophers and sanguinary
triflers.' When this viewpoint is dominant, the sympathies
withheld from both conservatives and radicals are directed

towards Razumov, as the helpless tool of them both. But although it is in fact true that Razumov is exploited by both sides of the political struggle, as a double-agent used by both Councillor Mikulin and the anarchists, it is also noticeable that a good deal less attention is directed towards his role as an unwilling agent of autocracy. What we see, in the main, is his destruction at the hands of the radicals; and in this sense, the novel's official thesis of 'neutrality', disparaging both parties alike, is in practice dominated by a second attitude: its anti-revolutionary bias. There is this interesting comment, for example, on the interviews during which Councillor Mikulin converts Razumov into his spy:

> To the morality of a Western reader an account of these meetings would wear perhaps the sinister character of old legendary tales where the Enemy of Mankind is represented holding subtly mendacious dialogue with some tempted soul. It is not my part to protest. Let me but remark that the Evil One, with his single passion for satanic pride for the only motive, is yet, on a larger, modern view, allowed to be not quite so black as he used to be painted. With what greater latitude, then, should we appraise the exact shade of mere mortal man, with his many passions and his miserable ingenuity in error, always dazzled by the base glitter of mixed motives, everlastingly betrayed by a short-sighted wisdom.

The novel's usual appeal to the inscrutable alienness of Russian morality is here significantly reversed: we are asked instead to relate the event to our own, tolerantly English understanding of error and complexity. The result is to make Mikulin's manipulative tactics appear less reprehensible than they really are: but it is observable that no such leniency of judgement is extended, elsewhere in the novel, to the actions of the anarchists. Mikulin is certainly criticised as an autocrat, but he is not caricatured; and to this extent, 'neutrality' once more suffers.

The treatment of Razumov himself is one of the most striking examples of the novel's ambiguities of feeling. 'Razumov', says Conrad, 'is treated sympathetically. Why should he not be? He is an ordinary young man, with a healthy capacity for work and sane ambitions. He has an average conscience. If he is slightly abnormal it is only in his sensitiveness to his position.' As a judgement on Razumov before his encounter with Haldin, this seems accurate enough: we are told that he is an amiable and generous man with 'an instinctive hold on normal, practical, everyday life'. But it is difficult to see how a man of this kind—'ordinary', 'average', and only 'slightly' abnormal—could have grown so rapidly into the cruel, arrogant, malicious egoist whom the novel actually presents. There is a tension between what the novel shows us of Razumov and what it says of him: and the latter portrayal is a good deal more admirable than the former. The truth is that the novel, in pointing out reasons for genuine sympathy with its protagonist—his loneliness, his previously attractive character, his reasonable ambitions and their tragic collapse— lulls us at the same time into a tolerant attitude towards his less engaging traits: his violence, selfish cynicism and autocratic sneering. The formal motive for this leniency is, once again, the need for neutrality:

> That I should . . . mention again that Mr Razumov's youth had no one in the world, as literally no one as it can be honestly affirmed of any human being, is but a statement of fact from a man who believes in the psychological value of facts. There is also, perhaps, a desire of punctilious fairness.

But the strategic gain of this punctilious fairness is to render Razumov more effective as a focus for criticism of the revolutionaries: the novel indulges in Razumov qualities which it criticises in them, and so gives him a title to judge them. Razumov's 'extremism'—his morbid unbalanced cynicism—is half-excused by an appeal to his tragic situation: his loneliness and victimisation:

> (Laspara) raised his arm and went on. Razumov backed against the low wall, looked after him, spat violently, and went on his way with an angry mutter—
> 'Cursed Jew!'

He did not know anything about it. Julius Laspara might have been a Transylvanian, a Turk, an Andalusian, or a citizen of one of the Hanse towns for anything he could tell to the contrary. But this is not a story of the West, and this exclamation must be recorded, accompanied by the comment that it was merely an expression of hate and contempt, best adapted to the nature of the feelings Razumov suffered from at the time.

By withdrawing into its posture of 'Western eyes' detachment, the passage avoids too damaging a criticism of Razumov. His foreignness is drawn on as a point in his favour: what may appear unpleasantly violent to an Englishman is excusable, because inscrutable, in a Russian. In this sense, then, the narrator's restricted and conventional viewpoint half-endorses Razumov's anti-revolutionary attitude, under the thin guise of neutrality: the refusal to judge results in a covert confirmation of his judgement. It is worth comparing this with the narrator's response to the sight of Peter Ivanovitch and Madame de S—— driving together, as a couple of grotesque figures, in their carriage:

But it is a vain enterprise for sophisticated Europe to try and understand these doings. Considering the air of gravity extending even to the physiognomy of the coachman and the action of the showy horses, this quaint display might have possessed a mystic significance, but to the corrupt frivolity of a Western mind, like my own, it seemed hardly decent.

The priggishness of 'hardly decent' belongs to the narrator, not to Conrad, but his attitude is nevertheless supported; the appeal to 'Western eyes' is here, very clearly, intended to be taken as ironic. The alienness which half-excuses Razumov's behaviour is not appealed to in the case of his anarchist opponents.

What is in fact at work, in the relationship between the narrator and Razumov, is a kind of double-detachment. Both men are politically disengaged, but to the extent that both take their stand, if anywhere, on 'practical, everyday life', they share a common, anti-revolutionary front. In this sense there is a good deal of Razumov in the narrator himself (as there is, quite evidently, in Conrad); but in order to avoid commitment to the cynicism and negation which underpin Razumov's detachment, the narrator must in turn detach himself from this position, stressing the Russian's inscrutability. By doing so, he can protect the 'sanity' of his own decent English empiricism from the risks of a corrosive scepticism; but having established that defensive margin between himself and scepticism, he can then, through the character of Razumov, indulge it to the full, in a way which severely criticises his own 'decent' conventionality. The novel, by the use of its narrator-device, can therefore satirise the limits of English empiricism by the protrayal of passionate experience beyond its scope, without permitting that empirical position to be undermined; it can indulge, through Razumov, a wholly un-English nihilism without allowing that stance to be fully affirmed. Razumov's foreignness allows the narrator to distance himself protectively from his 'extremism', but the extremism is often no more than a matter of tone:

> Who could have written about him in that letter from Petersburg? A fellow-student, surely—some imbecile victim of revolutionary propaganda, some foolish slave of foreign, subversive ideas. . . . He smiled inwardly at the absolute wrongheadedness of the whole thing, the self-deception of a criminal idealist shattering his existence like a thunderclap out of a clear sky, and re-echoing amongst the wreckage in the false assumptions of these other fools.

The language here—'imbecile', 'criminal', 'fools'—is undoubtedly Razumov's; but it differs only in its ferocity from the novel's own viewpoint. In so far as Razumov's passionate intensity reveals him as part of the mysterious 'Russian soul', he slips, like Miss Haldin, beyond the borders of the narrator's comprehension, and so is safely distanced from English experience; but since he also slips beyond the borders of the narrator's criticism, the judgement which his 'noble' intensity implies on the timidities of England is allowed to stand.

In this sense, indeed, what is operative in the novel is not a double but a treble-detachment. In a spiral of overlapping ironies, the narrator detaches himself from Razumov's *dégagement,* and the novel in turn detaches itself from its own narrator. At the climax of the novel, when Razumov confesses his act of betrayal to Miss Haldin, the narrator is objectified within his own narrative:

> . . . standing thus before each other in the glaring light, between the four bare walls, they seemed brought out from the confused immensity of the Eastern borders to be exposed cruelly to the observation of my Western eyes. And I observed them. There was nothing else to do. My existence seemed so utterly forgotten by these two that I dared not now make a movement. . . .

At the crisis of the interview, Razumov turns on the narrator:

> Slowly his sullen eyes moved in my direction. 'How did this old man come here?' he muttered, astounded.

The point of this dramatic highlighting of the language-teacher's irrelevance is crucial to the novel's intentions. In so far as both he and Razumov oppose revolution from a 'practical' standpoint, they have a common viewpoint; but just as it is detrimental to English decency for the narrator to be too closely identified with Razumov, so it is damaging to the heroic 'nobility' which Razumov comes to embody for it to be associated with the cautious conventionality of the old man. The narrator is instinctively unsympathetic to revolution, but since his judgement is the reflection of a characteristic English narrowness, it counts (as he is the first to acknowledge) for little; it must therefore be overriden by the judgement of a man who shares all the mysterious intensity of Russia and is yet himself politically conservative. Razumov, in other words, stands midway between anarchists and narrator: he has both the passionate 'soul' of the first and the 'normal, practical, everyday' scepticism of the second. Through him, a criticism of social revolution can be achieved which escapes the damaging corollary of a rigid incomprehension of human passions.

Officially, this is once more part of the novel's effort at neutrality: Conrad strives to hold in balance a degree of pity for Razumov and a sense of his alienness. In fact, that alienness finally works to confirm the book's political bias: if Razumov, a Russian sensitive to the issues which lie at the roots of anarchist action, is himself hostile to political change, then the conventional wisdom of English conservatism, as embodied in the narrator, is fundamentally confirmed. The narrator is criticised, and this, again, would seem to contribute to 'balance': yet he is criticised not for his views, but for his lack of a dimension of inward experience which would, ironically, merely confirm those views at a 'profounder' level.

The point of the spiral of ironies, partial views, disclaimers and reservations which forms the structure of *Under Western Eyes* is to sustain a precariously fine tension between 'English' and 'foreign' experience. The provincial pragmatism of English culture is sharply exposed, in the light of foreign currents of feeling with which it cannot deal; the English expatriate abroad is revealed as impotent. At the same time, the flaws of that foreign experience—its ruthless intensities and destructive impersonality—are contrasted with the kindliness and sensitivity of the English liberal. Yet the 'balance' is not quite so reciprocal as that account of it would suggest. For the true conflict within the novel is not between English conservatism and foreign revolutionism: it is between English conservatism and foreign 'spirit'. What is admired, in Nathalie Haldin and Sophia Antonovna, is a 'nobility of soul' which remains, in the end, conveniently indeterminate: relatable to any time, place or action. By abstracting that 'spirit' from the particular political projects within which it is realised, English culture can be satirised for its paucity of passionate imagination without its actual assumptions being at all undermined. The 'style' of Russian existence—its 'mystic' inwardness and dramatic poetry —is used to criticise the inert pieties of England; yet when it goes beyond a matter of style to a question of its political embodiments, assent is quickly withdrawn. It is the women anarchists—Tekla, Nathalie, Sophia—who are admired, for what they symbolise are essentially qualities of 'being'; the men who wish to realise those qualities in action are frauds or freaks.

Conrad, of course, was continuously preoccupied with a conflict between the structures of English rationality and kinds of experience which those structures failed to encompass. What is interesting about *Under Western Eyes* is the unique ambivalence of this conflict, directly registered in the structure of the novel. It is, at base, an ambivalence which suggests a profound uncertainty in attitude: an uncertainty which is projected into, and half-concealed by, the 'scrupulous impartiality' which the novel strives to sustain. That impartiality is meant to suggest a neutral balance between conservative and anarchist, yet it is more than once disturbed by an uncontrolled impulse to caricature the latter; it is meant to indicate the limits of English pragmatism, yet it does this only in a way which leaves that pragmatism essentially confirmed. *Under Western Eyes*, like many of Conrad's works, contrasts the structures of civilised thought with alien experience; but whereas in other of his novels there is a genuine dialectic between the two, so that alien experience is allowed radically to question civilised structures which in turn gain fresh validation from the encounter, no such dialectic is really present here. It appears to be there, but disappears on analysis. In this novel, the foreign reality of Russia is not ultimately allowed to undermine the Western attitudes of the narrator; it reveals the limits of those attitudes, but, precisely because it is a *foreign* reality, recedes then into a distant, inscrutable realm which presents no active challenge to conventional English wisdom. The English narrator and the Russian revolutionaries live in different worlds, and that, really, is all there is to say; there is no question of either world gaining a point of critical purchase upon the other. The posture of neutrality—the bemused recognition that Orientals are different—is at one point a target for satire; but at another point it helps to keep the revolutionary world safely at arm's length. That deliberate distancing is evident, as we have seen, in the caricature of the anarchists, which is a symptom of the refusal to allow English experience to be effectively questioned. Since it is Razumov, and not the narrator, who provides us with these parodic descriptions of revolutionaries, the narrator's 'neutrality' is preserved; but since much of his narrative dramatises the thoughts of a virulently anti-revolutionary Russian, it is not preserved at the expense of castigating radicalism.

In all these ways, *Under Western Eyes* is a significant novel from the viewpoint of this study. Its central concern is with the relations between English and foreign experience: and its official viewpoint is one of strict neutrality towards them both. What leads one in the first place to suspect that neutrality is the novel's handling of both Razumov and the revolutionaries; and when the partialities of that handling have been seen, it is apparent that the pose of neutrality is, at base, a device for permitting Russian experience to satirise, but not to concretely question, the assumptions on which the English narrator works. In his greatest work, Conrad was able to transcend those English assumptions, achieving a vantage-point beyond them from which they could be probed and illuminated; in this novel, the formal structure of that transcendence is present, but its content is strangely lacking. To that extent, *Under Western Eyes* is relevant to a problem which will be raised continually throughout this study: the problem of a kind of novel which can neither fully accept, nor fully escape, the conventions and habits of its own culture.

That final reservation, however, is significant: it defines the essential distinction between Walsh's subversive nihilism and Clarissa's capacity to subdue her anti-social insights to the requirements of the social game. Walsh refuses this tactic; he is 'careless of all these damned proprieties', bitterly resentful of Clarissa's absorption into the destructive falsities of Society life. 'The obvious thing to say of her was that she was worldly; cared too much for rank and society and getting on in the world—which was true in a sense; she had admitted it to him.' But that candid admission, while counting against Clarissa, is also meant to protect her from a charge of unreflective superficiality. She is part of the upper-class world, despite the unorthodox emotional and intellectual preoccupations she has in common with Walsh; yet because of those preoccupations, she is 'spiritually' superior to the Hugh Whitbreads who compose her milieu. As a character, then, Mrs Dalloway is ambivalent: she is conscious, like Walsh, of an undermining purposelessness at the core of her party which crystallises around a guest's chance reference to death ('Oh! thought Clarissa, in the middle of my party, here's death she thought'); yet she displays at the same time that intense concern with fashionable success which Walsh finds most repellent. 'She did think it mattered, her party, and it made her feel quite sick to know that it was all going wrong.' Her response to the whole episode is thus significantly uncertain: 'Every time she gave a party she had this feeling of being something not herself, and that everyone was unreal in one way; much more real in another'.

There is, then, a quality of Walsh's social viewpoint in Mrs Dalloway; yet that viewpoint is restrained from becoming dominant by the handling of Walsh himself. He is able to register a radical criticism because he is, literally, an outsider, having spent some years out of England. 'All India lay behind him; plains, mountains; epidemics of cholera; a district twice as big as Ireland; decisions he had come to alone. . . .' Walsh, a rootless expatriate in a wilderness of London drawing-rooms, has encountered a reality alien to that life, in the exigencies of

CHAPTER II

Evelyn Waugh and the Upper-class Novel

I

Lord, lord, the snobbery of the English! thought Peter Walsh,
standing in the corner. How they loved dressing up in gold
lace and doing homage! That must be—by Jove it was—Hugh
Whitbread, snuffing around the precincts of the great . . .
hoarding secrets which he would die to defend, though it was
only some little piece of tittle-tattle dropped by a court foot-
man. . . . God knows, the rascals who get hanged for battering
the brains of a girl out in a train do less harm on the whole
than Hugh Whitbread and his kindness! Look at him now, on
tiptoe, dancing forward, bowing and scraping, as the Prime
Minister and Lady Bruton emerged. . . .

THE scene is Clarissa Dalloway's party at the end of Virginia
Woolf's *Mrs Dalloway*; and Walsh is the caustic, excluded,
hypercritical observer of its empty glitter. As such, he is the
means—the only means, indeed, in the novel—whereby a
trenchant social criticism can be effectively focused on the
shimmering futility of the upper-class world of which Clarissa
is symbol.

To a strictly limited extent, it is a criticism which the novel
itself endorses. Clarissa herself, for all her cultivated social
aplomb, shares Walsh's sense of an ultimate pointlessness in the
light of which upper-class society reveals itself as absurdly
unreal:

Oddly enough, she was one of the most thorough-going sceptics
he had ever met, and possibly . . . she said to herself, As we are
a doomed race . . . as the whole thing is a bad joke, let us, at
any rate, do our part; mitigate the sufferings of our fellow-
prisoners . . . decorate the dungeon with flowers and air-
cushions; be as decent as we possibly can.

the Indian service; and this foreign standpoint contributes to his irritated dislike of Society charades. Yet by the same token it brands him as a 'cranky', querulous deviant from his social class, a broken and pathetic nomad, and to this extent qualifies the objective validity of his dissent. Through him, the novel can make a gesture towards a mysterious hinterland of experience barred to the fashionable world; yet because that hinterland remains merely nominal, suggestible only in the cryptic notation of the above quotation, it can be brought into no precise relation with upper-class society. Walsh, in any case, is also portrayed as a 'bookish' ex-socialist, and so is easily categorisable as the kind of intellectual for whom it is wise, in an honoured upper-class tradition, to reserve a slight, pitying contempt. The only character in *Mrs Dalloway* who might furnish an articulate critique of Clarissa's world is therefore significantly muted by the manner of his presentation. He is also in love with Clarissa: a fact which both tempers the severity of his criticism and suggests a subjective rather than objective motive for it. He sees her as tainted, through her marriage to Richard Dalloway, with 'a great deal of the public-spirited, British Empire, tariff-reform, governing-class spirit', but a private antagonism to Dalloway enters into this accusation as an emotional factor, and he himself has no alternative to offer Clarissa beyond the intellectual disillusions of a rootless, middle-aged seediness.

Mrs Dalloway, then, is protected by the novel from the full force of the damaging charges which might be listed against her. She is, her friend Sally Seton remarks, a snob: yet while this is true enough, as her extraordinary flow of reverential piety at the sight of the Queen's car sufficiently illustrates, Sally's judgement is not allowed to stand:

> And so (Sally) would go on, Peter felt, hour after hour . . . people thought she had married beneath her; her five sons; and what was the other thing—plants, hydrangeas, syringas, very rare hibiscus lilies that never grow north of the Suez Canal, but she, with one gardener in a suburb near Manchester, had beds of them, positively beds!

Sally's charge of snobbery merely rationalises her own 'provincial' resentment, itself (with the 'placing' reference to the Manchester suburb) snobbishly characterised by the novel. Woolf's whole attitude to snobbery is, in fact, interestingly ambiguous:

> For there was Professor Brierly, who lectured on Milton, talking to little Jim Hutton (who was unable even for a party like this to compass both tie and waistcoat or make his hair lie flat) and even at this distance they were quarrelling, she could see. For Professor Brierly was a very queer fish . . . his innocence blent with snobbery; he quivered if made conscious, by a lady's unkempt hair, a youth's boots, of an underworld, very creditable doubtless, of rebels, of ardent young people. . . . Professor Brierly (Clarissa could see) wasn't hitting it off with little Jim Hutton (who wore red socks, his black being at the laundery). . . .

The passage displays a broad-minded satiric amusement at the Professor's fussy traditionalism (he is an academic, and so both inside and outside Society), while thoroughly endorsing his contempt for 'little' Jim Hutton, with his unspeakable gaffes. Here, as elsewhere in the novel, the social conventions of the English upper class are criticised and upheld at the same time.

This last passage from *Mrs Dalloway*, trivial as it is in its context, expresses an important truth about the world of Woolf's novels in particular and the English upper-class novel in general. *Mrs Dalloway* is 'emancipated' enough to satirise the more obvious pieties and rigidities of upper-class English society: it can see, as Professor Brierly cannot, a value in the rebellion and ardour of an unorthodox underworld, and that ardour can reduce a concern with ties and waistcoats to its proper triviality. The particular underworld of Woolf's novels is a realm of aesthetic hedonism and flamboyant individualism which is alien to the more conventional habits of upper-class life, and potentially subversive of their assumptions. Most of Woolf's central characters reach beyond the limits of their habitual social contexts towards attitudes which those limits cannot easily accommodate. The formal upper-class world operates by tradition, empiricism, permanence, unquestioned practice, public spirit; the underworld of Woolf's liberal spirits centres on timeless intensities, contemplative privacy, 'metaphysical' probings, the shifting relativism of subjective judgement. Between these two realms, then, there is bound to be severe tension: the disparity, in fact, between Mr and Mrs Ramsay in *To The Lighthouse*.

Yet the underworld, even when hostile or indifferent to formal upper-class culture, is structurally a part of it. The ethic of aesthetic individualism is a privileged one, dependent on a settled structure of wealth and leisure to protect it from the exigencies of work, hardship, responsibility, conformism. In this sense, the liberal scepticism of Woolf's emancipated aesthetes is not entirely unconstrained: it stops short, necessarily, at a radical questioning of the social structure on which, as a philosophy, it is parasitic. The frontiers of high society may be transcended in spirit, but they can hardly be transcended in fact; Professor Brierly may be satirised, but not at the risk of an alliance with the unorthodoxies of the contemptible Jim Hutton. The values of Woolf's novels, then, are at one point deviations from established upper-class life, at another point reflections of it. In *Mrs Dalloway*, the two modes can combine in a passage such as this:

> Clarissa guessed; Clarissa knew of course; she had seen something white, magical, circular, in the footman's hand, a disc inscribed with a name,—the Queen's, the Prince of Wales's, the Prime Minister's?—which by force of its lustre, burnt its way through (Clarissa saw the car diminishing, disappearing), to blaze among candelabras, glittering stars, breasts stiff with oak leaves, Hugh Whitbread and all his colleagues, the gentlemen of England, that night in Buckingham Palace.

Here it is the imagery and insignia of social privilege which furnish the material for a characteristically 'intense' complex of aesthetic perceptions. The established social order, here as elsewhere in the novel, itself becomes a source of heightened sensuous awareness, and the aesthetic and socially conventional accordingly reconciled.

The radical dependence of liberal, exploratory living on a firmly consolidated class-structure is a major theme of E. M. Forster's *Howard's End*. The personalist values of the Schlegel sisters can lead to the 'sloppiness' of a nervelessly whimsical sentimentality; they therefore need to be stiffened by the discipline, character-building and active masculinity of the Wilcoxes. The central contradiction which the novel dramatises, that is to say, is the one *within* the upper middle class: a conflict between its liberal humanist deviants, gentle, perceptive but impotent, and its energetically philistine economic architects. Forster is shrewd enough to perceive the degree to which his own upper-class liberalism is parasitic on the social structure it criticises: in this respect, as in others, he is a more honest and consistent liberal than Virginia Woolf. If liberalism is to take seriously its values of freely unrestricted exploration, it must at some point bring its flexibly disinterested inquiry to bear on the problem of its own social basis. And this is what *Howard's End* attempts. Unfortunately, Forster is not shrewd enough to recognise that he is faced here with an insoluble contradiction: and his inability (or refusal) to acknowledge this is the primary reason for the novel's failure. It fails because it is faked, in an effort to evade the intractable problem of its own subject-matter.

The truth is that the problem of reconciling 'inner' and 'outer' worlds, Monk and Beast, Schlegel and Wilcox, cannot be resolved at a merely formal level: resolved, that is, by a neatly efficient synthesis of the abstract qualities of one party with the abstract qualities of the other. What is in question, inescapably, is an open conflict of values in the real world, which cannot be blandly accommodated within a single, practical or conceptual framework. Yet it is itself a significant indication of Forster's Schlegel-like distance from the real world that he believes the problem amenable to such a formal solution. What is required is merely that the Wilcox virtues of 'grit' be grafted on to the Schlegel values of sensitivity; the fact that liberalism and authoritarianism, aestheticism and philistinism are inherently exclusive of one another is thus effectively concealed. This formalism itself encloses another: we are asked to evaluate, not the activities of the Wilcoxes, but their 'qualities': to look, not at the realities of economic exploitation, the creation of unemployment, determined opposition to welfare legislation, but at the quality of 'grit' to which these facts can be conveniently abstracted. The novel, of course, contains gestures of protest against the unreality of its own resolution: when Helen Schlegel describes the Wilcoxes as 'cosmopolitan dust and stink', a voice which has been deliberately muted throughout the narrative finally breaks irritably through. But it is not permitted to be heard; instead, we are asked to believe that the patently repulsive Henry Wilcox is 'lovable', as we are asked to recognise that the working-man Leonard Bast, despite all appearances to the contrary, is 'real'.

Bast, as most critics agree, is a mere cypher: he symbolises a realm of experience from which the Schlegel world is hopelessly estranged. What is most questionable about his presentation in the novel, however, is the implied equivalence between him and the Wilcoxes, from the viewpoint of the Schlegels. Both Bast and the Wilcoxes stand for 'real' life, in contrast to the Schlegels' contemplative world; yet it is only, once more, by a formalist attention to 'quality' rather than 'content' that such an attitude can be credibly maintained. For the Schlegels, Leonard Bast and Henry Wilcox constitute one sphere, while they themselves form a second; but the true antinomies, surely, are the single, if self-divided, world of the Schlegels and Wilcoxes on the one hand, and the patronised, exploited existence of Bast on the other. It is, indeed, only a curiously abstract imagination which could comprehend Bast and Wilcox within a single, 'economic' framework, thus sliding over the crucial, and more definitive, elements which divide them. It is this authentic grouping of interests which the novel comes slowly to recognise, in the marriage of Margaret Schlegel to Henry Wilcox and the accompanying death of Leonard. The upper middle-class families unite—although it is really less a 'synthesis' than a straight capitulation on the Schlegels' part; Bast lives on only in the conveniently symbolic form of Helen's baby.

The problem of bringing its own, partial and specialised experience into some effective relation with the wider social existence which surrounds it is a persistent one for the upper-class novel. In *A Passage To India*, Forster, as a liberal, rejects the imperialist solutions: the assumption that traditional English values must be either protected against, or made to predominate over, the shifting tide of anonymous experience which is India. Yet the fact that common reality is seen in this way, as amorphous, alien and opaque, has its own significance. The liberal humanism of Mrs Moore rejects the formal upper-class ideology of her son; yet in so far as the alternative is an instinctive empathy with India which confirms a sense of futility, it is, in the end, a humanism structurally related to the satirised orthodoxies of Anglo-India. The falsity of that ideology can be exposed, but only at the expense of undermining all objective value; once 'civilised' values (actually, of course, the values of a particular social class within civilisation) have proved empty, the consequence is a sickening contingency in all human life.

It is possible, perhaps, to bridge the gap between this attitude of Mrs Moore's and the world of Evelyn Waugh by a comment on a novelist who shares to an acute degree the sense of 'panic and emptiness' of the first, and the sophisticated high society satire of the second. There is a point in Aldous Huxley's *Antic Hay* where the modish absurdities of the upper-class set are ruptured by a 'dramatic' interpolation:

> 'We'd better be going. Goodness knows what's happening behind us.' He indicated with a little movement of the head the loiterers around the coffee-stall. 'Some disturbance among the *canaille*.'

Mrs Viveash looked round. The cab-drivers and the other consumers of midnight coffee had gathered in an interested circle, curious and sympathetic, round the figure of a woman who was sitting, like a limp bundle tied up in black cotton and mackintosh, on the stall-keeper's high stool, leaning wearily against the walls of the booth. A man stood beside her drinking tea out of a thick white cup. . . .

The old woman has collapsed from hunger and exhaustion, and Gumbril, the novel's hero, is alone among his friends in feeling the horror of the event:

'It's appalling, it's horrible,' said Gumbril at last, after a long, long silence, during which he had, indeed, been relishing to the full the horror of it all. Life, don't you know.

'Life, don't you know' is Huxley's comment, not Gumbril's, and its hard-boiled flippancy is meant to satirise the befuddlement of Gumbril's indignation. Yet Huxley himself, beneath the flippancy, is really as befuddled, offering no sort of constructive response beyond a vague guilt. The incident occurs, but nothing can be done with it: it is merely one more symptom of an obscure malaise, 'some profound mysterious wound in the world's side'. There is no attempt to relate the fact of poverty to the social system which permits Gumbril and his friends their privileged fantasy-lives: responsibility for the old couple's plight lies not in a particular social order but in the nature of things. The feelings the episode evokes in Gumbril are significantly akin to the pangs of unrequited love: all forms of deprivation merge indiscriminately into one. And so the novel, in a way we shall examine in early Waugh, can criticise its own social environment without taking up an identifiably alternative standpoint. Rose, the innocent girl drawn into the upper-class world, is used to satirise Gumbril's decadent friends, but they are used in turn to satirise Rose's callow social pretensions; the bourgeois aestheticism of Mercaptan is heavily attacked by Lypiatt, but Lypiatt himself, the moral castigator of a corrupt society, is a ranting utopian foreigner. It is these two elements of *Antic Hay*—a sense of disintegration which, because it seems 'metaphysical', does not impinge too closely on the established social order, and a satirical technique which is opportunistic rather than consistently angled—which we can now examine in the work of Evelyn Waugh.

II

The subject-matter of Evelyn Waugh's first novel, *Decline and Fall*, is seen through the eyes of the novel's hero Paul Pennyfeather; but 'hero' is rather too emphatic a term, as Waugh himself comments in the course of the narrative. The whole of the book, he remarks, is 'really an account of the mysterious disappearance of Paul Pennyfeather, so that readers must not complain if the shadow which took his name does not amply fill the important part of hero for which he was originally cast'.

The 'shadowy' quality of Pennyfeather is central to Waugh's intentions in *Decline and Fall*. Paul is a neutral, wholly unrealised focal-point upon the reality the novel presents: he is passive, inert and uncritical, registering no kind of attitude to his own experience. His most typical feature is a sort of blankness: when Margot Beste-Chetwynde announces her intention of ditching him for a more successful man, he is 'greatly pained at how little he was pained. . . .' At the same time Pennyfeather, partly because of this shadowy half-presence, emerges as less eccentric, more decently 'normal', than the high society caricatures among whom he moves. His normality is a negative quality—really nothing more than a lack of any notable quirks in a world of grotesque figures—but it impels us towards a half-conscious identification with his progress, for want of an alternative viewpoint. He is, for instance, notably more 'moral' than other characters, even though that morality is satirised as a form of callowness: when he is asked to say why he has been sent down from Oxford he resolves, 'true to his training', upon honesty.

The significance of Paul's blankness is twofold. It allows the novel's real concerns—the life of upper-class society—to emerge 'objectively', as a neutrally descriptive record rather than as part of a more personal, inward, evaluative history; and it deftly prevents this experience from being unduly criticised by the man who is its sacrificial victim. Paul has been sent down unjustly from Oxford and is sentenced to seven years' penal servitude as scapegoat for Margot Beste-Chetwynde's crimes of prostitution and white slave traffic; but his inability to belong to his own experience prevents him from articulating anything remotely approaching a protest. When he does finally reveal an attitude, in the meditative quiet of his prison-cell, it goes to endorse the system which has used him. He is torn between two principles:

On one side was the dead weight of precept, inherited from generations of schoolmasters and divines. According to these, the problem was difficult but not insoluble. He had 'done the right thing' in shielding the woman: so much was clear, but Margot had not quite filled the place assigned to her, for in this case she was grossly culpable, and he was shielding her, not from misfortune or injustice, but from the consequence of her crimes . . . he had wrestled with this argument without achieving any satisfactory result except a growing conviction that there was something radically inapplicable about this whole code of ready-made honour that is the still, small voice, trained to command, of the Englishman all the world over. On the other hand was the undeniable cogency of Peter Beste-Chetwynde's 'You can't see Mamma in prison, can you?' The more Paul considered this, the more he perceived it to be a statement of a natural law . . . he saw the *impossibility* of Margot in prison; the bare connexion of vocables associating the ideas was obscene. Margot dressed in prison uniform . . . these things were *impossible.* . . .

The conflict—it is, as we shall see, common in Waugh—is essentially between a sense of morality and a sense of style. The morality of 'schoolmasters and divines' by which Margot might be condemned is naïvely inadequate to the true, less clumsily categorisable complexities of the situation. The code, however, is not explicitly rejected: there is 'something' radically inapplicable about it, but it is a matter of feeling rather than formulation. What overrides that morality is a sense of taste and stylistic fitness, which leads to the endorsement of an *Übermensch* morality for the rich, but not in a way which involves a direct stand on snobbish privilege. It is not that the rich should not, in theory, be punished, just that the very notion is impossible to entertain, and so unreal. The passage can thus take up a wholly indefensible attitude without (as would happen, probably, in later Waugh) taking a principled stand on privileged inequality, since this would be to declare too openly an admiring attitude towards the aristocracy, and so disturb the carefully clinical 'neutrality' of the novel's tone. Indeed, the attitude can even posture as a sort of radicalism:

> If someone had to suffer that the public might be discouraged from providing poor Mrs Grimes with the only employment for which civilisation had prepared her, then it had better be Paul than (Margot), for anyone who has been to an English public school will always feel comparatively at home in a prison. It is the people brought up in the gay intimacy of the slums, Paul learned, who find prison so soul-destroying.

Mrs Grimes is one of the girls whom Margot has shipped to a South American brothel; the reference to her covertly half-excuses the act, and so implicitly validates Paul's condoning attitude, by a brief, opportunistic parade of moral indignation which shifts the burden of responsibility from Margot herself on to a neatly abstract 'civilisation'. The novel thus manages to suggest a half-apology for white slave traffic under cover of a pretended 'humanitarianism'. The same attitude is extended in the following sentences: the connection of public school and prison is, of course, a familiar enough joke, but it also has its serious point, in presenting Paul's condonement of Margot's crimes as a self-sacrificial altruism which is again, in the 'knowingness' of the reference to the gay slum-dwellers, given its 'radical' tinge.

Paul, then, questions the traditional wisdom of the divines for what is offered as a subtler, more feeling response; his moral 'unorthodoxy' (he is rejecting 'Boy Scout honour' and doubting the 'still small voice' of Empire) thus gives a coating of stylish radicalism to what is in effect a thoroughly reactionary position. In taking this decision, then, Paul has moved away from the drably earnest, moralistic world of Potts, his Oxford intellectual friend, into a morality of style, and we are asked to see this as evidence of a sort of maturity. Yet it is also obvious enough that Paul has not wholly escaped the Boy Scout code: his condonement of the system which exploits him flouts that code at one point while confirming it at another. His moral conflict over Margot, and the self-sacrifice to which it leads, signify a seriousness and gentlemanly honour which no other character in the book would be capable of showing. And in this sense, Paul is still a butt of the novel's satire: we are asked to approve, on the whole, of his attitude towards Margot, but also to see the solemn absurdity of the love-struck heroism which motivates it. In a characteristic Waugh manœuvre, the novel endorses Paul's position on one level while satirising him for it on another; as a result, it sidesteps a serious condemnation of high society while simultaneously suggesting how deluded Paul really is, in the light of Margot's callous behaviour. Endorsement and condemnation cancel each other out into the blank which is Paul Pennyfeather.

There is a similar ambiguity in Paul's final retreat to Oxford and holy orders. He began, in the opening chapters of the book, as an inexperienced, morally serious but not priggish youth; he is drawn into upper-class life, but drawn into it at an ambiguous point, neither fully inward with nor wholly external to its typical behaviour. He is external enough to be used by the novel as a neutral focus on that world, but sufficiently inward with it not to act as a critic. He occupies an indeterminate place midway between the Beste-Chetwyndes and Potts, the dedicated exposer of upper-class vice. His decision to shield Margot from the consequences of her crimes reveals the extent to

which he has identified himself with her world, in contrast to
the drearily distasteful realm of ordinary morality and intellectual effort; but at the same time, that decision detaches him
from Society into the isolation of the victim. His moral gesture
saves Margot, but also reveals him as an 'outsider', too passive,
gentlemanly and serious to survive in the jungle of Mayfair.
Paul, then, is approved for his honour, but also, finally, satirised
for it. His honour leaves him stranded, jettisoned from the
upper-class world; and there is nowhere to go but to withdraw into a monastic intellectualism. Since this, with its
'amusing' seriousness about ideas and social responsibility, is
the target of Waugh's satire, Paul's withdrawal from Society
does not count too heavily against Society itself. His mistake,
according to Professor Silenus, has simply been to get involved:

> Now you're a person who was clearly meant to stay in the seats
> and sit still and if you get bored watch the others. Somehow
> you got on to the wheel, and you got thrown off again at once
> with a hard bump. It's all right for Margot, who can cling on,
> and for me, at the centre, but you're static. Instead of this absurd
> division into sexes they ought to class people as static and dyna-
> mic. . . . What was it I came back for? . . .Oh, yes, of course.
> I know of no more utterly boring and futile occupation than
> generalising about life. . . .

The image of the wheel is intended to neutralise what we have
seen in the novel to the status of an automatic and unquestionable game; the Professor's final words then detach him from
this detachment. Because society is a game, the novel's attitude
of uncommitted satire—its bored watching of others—can be
maintained; but to maintain it involves blurring any critical
judgement of Margot and her kind. It is just that some are fitted
for the game and others are not. 'You know, Paul,' says Peter
Beste-Chetwynde at the end of the book, 'I think it was a
mistake you ever got mixed up with us; don't you? We're
different somehow. Don't quite know how.'

The humour of Waugh's early satire works, in general, by
a bland externality which reduces violent, grotesque and night-

marish events to the status of casual asides. The consequence of this is interestingly paradoxical. At first glance, it gives the impression of a kind of control: the novel remains serenely un-ruffled by the violent fantasies it records, filtering them through a level, dispassionate tone which creates a comic tension between substance and form. In some ways, this tone is the equivalent, at a literary level, of a quality common to Waugh's characters: an inability to be surprised or disoriented by experience which is partly the sophisticated Englishman's bland self-possession, partly a sense that nothing that happens is ever real enough to warrant significant response. The two attitudes interact in the subject-matter of the novels, so that bored sophistication comes very close to a more troubling sense of blank futility and dis-possession; but they interact also in the novel's own approach to this subject-matter. For the scrupulous neutrality which im-plies a kind of control on the novelist's part is really an illusion: it is essentially a way of concealing a more deep-seated lack of control, an inability to interpret, evaluate and understand the experience recorded. It is therefore difficult to determine whether the novels present a deliberately external attitude to what is in some sense 'real' experience, or whether they merely register the inherent externality of unreal events. On the one hand there is this, familiar device in *Decline and Fall*:

> 'She is the honourable Mrs Beste-Chetwynde, you know—sister-in-law of Lord Pastmaster—a very wealthy woman, South American. They always say that she poisoned her hus-band, but of course little Beste-Chetwynde doesn't know that. It never came into court, but there was a great deal of talk about it at the time. Perhaps you remember the case?'
> 'No,' said Paul.
> 'Powdered glass,' said Flossie shrilly, 'in his coffee.'
> 'Turkish coffee,' said Dingy.

This is merely gratuitous: there is no 'real' event to be responded to, since the related incident exists wholly at the level of lan-guage. It is just a piece of opportunism, on a level with the casually reported amputation of Lord Tangent's leg, to inject

a momentary, uninterpreted sensationalism into the narrative.
On the other hand, there is the outcome of Paul's trial:

> His sentence of seven years' penal servitude was rather a blow.
> 'In ten years she will be worn out,' he thought as he drove in
> the prison van to Blackstone Gaol.

The humour of this depends at least in part upon our taking
the prison-sentence seriously—as 'real'—and then constrasting
it with Paul's understated response; the violence which was
merely abstract in the case of the powdered glass suddenly
assumes a more sinisterly concrete form. This, indeed, is the
irony: the violence and fraud which amused us at a distance
now enter the foreground of the novel, to catch us unawares.

Yet it is difficult to believe that Paul's experience in prison
is really very different in quality from the amputation of Tangent's leg or the clichéd fantasy which surrounds the butler
Philbrick. The prison is really a joke, the processes of law are
'preposterous', and Paul finds his weeks of confinement to be
among the happiest of his life: 'there was no need to shave, no
hesitation about what tie he should wear, none of the fidgeting
with studs and collars and links that so distracts the waking
moments of civilised man'. So the novel is ambivalent in its
attitude towards Pennyfeather's incarceration: on the one hand
it is the unexpected eruption of a violent undertow of reality
into an unreal social world; on the other hand, it shares in the
fantasy qualities of that world, and so can offer no genuine
criticism of it. The most it does is poke gentle fun at cuff-links.

There is a similar ambivalence about the crime and fraud
within the upper-class world itself. Its point is to suggest the
real depredations and brutalities which underlie the glittering
surface Paul finds attractive, but the sharp edge of that criticism
is blunted by the grotesque enormity of the crimes themselves:
white slave traffic, poison, conspiracy. These forms of corruption are so extreme as to be unreal: they reflect less a considered satiric criticism than an uncontrolled sense of nightmare
and absurdity. In order to achieve a standpoint of 'moral'

criticism on the experience it presents, the novel needs to resort to a flamboyant and wholly incredible set of images, which merely share in the unreal quality of the society itself, and so are less effective as genuine criticisms in proportion to their monstrousness.

Decline and Fall, then, sets the keynote for many of Waugh's later themes. There is, to begin with, the conflict between morality and style, reflected in the vicissitudes of Pennyfeather's career. Pennyfeather, like Tony Last in *A Handful of Dust*, is a colourlessly honourable man in a stylish world of sharp operators; but although, like Last, he therefore represents the focal-point of a kind of social criticism, he resembles Last also in being too passive, unrealised and and inarticulate to make that criticism tell with any acuteness. The blankness which leads him to the role of victim also prevents him from reacting effectively against that role, and a radical questioning of an exploitative society is thus neatly avoided. The stylish world is predatory, but it has a verve and insouciance which is admired, in contrast to the monkish honesty of Pennyfeather himself. 'Morality' is not rejected, but it cannot survive relevantly within the realm of style; to be moral is to withdraw, perhaps rightly, from the world, but so to leave it invulnerable to one's criticisms. Endorsing and rejecting attitudes cancel each other out here, as they do elsewhere in the novel: Dr Fagan's educational commercialism is satirised, but so also are the progressive educational notions of Potts; both liberal and conservative responses to prison-reform are held up for ridicule; Negroes and racialists are found equally amusing; Potts the moral reformer is as absurd as the vices he hopes to abolish.

The upshot of all this is that upper-class values are satirised but not dismissed; they are fraudulent and hollow, but there is really nowhere else to turn. So the cool externality of the style is not, at root, a 'placing' externality at all: as a mode of perception, it is part of the world it sees. This fact is most evident in the garishly violent events of the novel, which find their epitome in the episode where Mr Prendergast is carved up with a handsaw. Like most of Waugh's grotesquely violent scenes, the incident is reported rather than presented, and this is itself significant: the imagery of violence is needed, as a shocking intimation of breakdown, but it must be enjoyed vicariously, through the accounts of eye-witnesses, so that it will not load the casually distanced reportage of the novel with a pressure it could not sustain. The surface-texture of flippant observation must be kept intact, but 'deeper' forces at the same time exposed. Yet 'exposure' implies a sort of controlled objectivity which is hardly there at all: the Prendergast incident, like other such occurrences in Waugh, is really a mixture of disturbance and indulgence. It is disturbance in so far as it indicates, not any significantly 'objective' reality in the novel (thematically, the event is wholly pointless), but an uncontrolled reflex of fantasy on the part of the novelist; it is indulgence in so far as it signifies a quite gratuitous sensationalism, done entirely for its own sake. In both ways, the neutrality of presentation is deceptive: it suggests a control which is not there. Paradoxically, Waugh's distance from the subject-matter of his satirical novels only goes to show how intimately a part of them he is: he resembles his characters most evidently in this inability to belong to his own experience.

Waugh's second novel, *Vile Bodies*, is similar in tone and technique to *Decline and Fall*, although it intensifies the earlier novel's mood: it is faster, more crowded and more openly disturbed, revolving on the chaotic images of motor-racing, parties and the movies. Events occur in a rapid fragmentation in which everything is at once ordinary and alarming; deaths, suicides and the fall of a government are caught up randomly in the general whirl. The society gossip-columnist Simon Balcairn is driven to suicide by the pressures of his career, but the event is too trivial to imply any indictment of the Society world: as a gesture, it has the histrionic unreality of the world it is rejecting. In the midst of this disintegration is the elusive figure of Father Rothschild, the mysteriously omniscient, inscrutably knowledgeable Jesuit. Father Rothschild is offered as a centre of spiritual value, but a centre which is necessarily suggestive rather than realised, alluding obscurely to some privileged access to significant truths and inside information. As with Paul Pennyfeather, moral value cannot be directly realised in the world; but Rothschild's worldly experience underlines the significance of his moral judgements. And since the precise nature of this worldly experience remains mysterious, we are supposed not to question his title to make judgements of this kind:

> 'Don't you think,' said Father Rothschild gently, 'that perhaps it is all in some way historical? I don't think people ever *want* to lose their faith either in religion or in anything else. I know very few young people, but it seems to me that they are all possessed with an almost fatal hunger for permanence. I think all these divorces show that. People aren't content just to muddle along nowadays. . . . And this word "bogus" they all use. . . . They won't make the best of a bad job nowadays. My private schoolmaster used to say, "If a thing's worth doing at all, it's worth doing well". . . . But these young people have got hold of another end of the stick, and for all we know it may be the right one. They say, "If a thing's not worth doing well, it's not worth doing at all".'

The collapse is 'historical', in the same sense that the fate of Mrs Grimes in *Decline and Fall* could be laid at the door of 'civilisation'. The whole comment is hedged with the disclaimers appropriate to most explicit moral reflections in Waugh (Father Rothschild 'knows very few young people', and later admits that 'it's all very difficult'), but the total effect is a masterpiece of disingenuous defence of the Bright Young Things, who gain, through this discernment of spiritual hunger in divorce statistics and Society slang, a wholly unrecognisable moral integrity. So the one respected moral spokesman of the novel, a man who significantly combines the innocent rectitude of Paul Pennyfeather with the worldly wisdom of the Beste-Chetwyndes, throws his spiritual weight behind the decaying upper-class world.

Like *Decline and Fall*, *Vile Bodies* contemplates a world which it can in no sense adequately interpret. Upper-class values are false, but the offered alternative is a vision of 'ordinary' life which is equally repugnant:

> Nina looked down and saw inclined at an odd angle a horizon of straggling red suburb; arterial roads dotted with little cars; factories, some of them working, others empty and decaying; a disused canal; some distant hills sown with bungalows; wireless masts and overhead power cables; men and women were indiscernible except as tiny spots; they were marrying and shopping and making money and having children. The scene lurched and tilted again as the aeroplane struck a current of air.
> 'I think I'm going to be sick,' said Nina.

The 'real' world is seen from the detachment of an aeroplane, tilted and distanced by the observer's standpoint to reduce it to an unreal 'scene', a framed and contemplated cinematic image which will dissolve and be replaced by others. The sense of giddiness and sickening disturbance, which is projected on to the observed scene, is in fact a quality of the observer's own 'unreal' vantage-point, suspended precariously in the spacious nothingness of air, vulnerable to shifting, random currents which distort perception and blot out reality. Nina feels sick, but the passage is significantly ambivalent about the cause: is it the scene she observes, or her own vertiginous viewpoint, which is responsible for the nausea? Is there an 'objective' emptiness in the world, or is the emptiness a quality of a way of seeing the world? The answer, in Waugh's case, is both: and this passage feels towards the obscure connection between an objective pointlessness in life and the neurosis of the Bright Young Things' behaviour. Yet the connection is deceptively established. In choosing to show the meaninglessness of a *suburban*, rather than upper-class environment, the novel implies a criticism of Society rootlessness—*they* do not marry, work, have children—while seeming at the same time to endorse this detachment by showing the 'real' world to be as empty as themselves. Thus the passage satirises Nina for her absurdly inadequate response to what she sees ('I think I'm going to be sick'), but also suggests that what she sees, from this privileged and distorting height, is the substantial truth of the ordinary world.

It is worth turning at this point from Waugh's two early satires to a more 'serious' novel, *A Handful of Dust*. The novel is judged serious because of its theme: it sets out to explore a contemporary mood of breakdown and futility in terms of the collapsing relationship of Tony and Brenda Last and the accompanying erosion of the country-house tradition of which Tony is representative. What is striking about *A Handful of Dust*, however, is that although the earlier satire is less in evidence, supposedly significant events and relationships are handled with the same one-dimensional externality as if the satire of *Decline and Fall* was in fact active. The novel offers an account of trivialised and insubstantial relationships; yet both qualities belong as much to its own technique as to its content. (In this respect, incidentally, the novel has more in common with *The Waste Land* than its title.) There is a sense in which the novel exploits the fact that it deals in 'objectively' vacuous relationships and responses to explain away its own superficiality of treatment. We are asked to believe that Brenda Last is in love with John Beaver: yet Beaver is even less present as a character than Paul Pennyfeather. The novel hinges on a 'deep' emotional crisis—the sudden death of the Lasts' son, John Andrew—yet it takes refuge in the upper-class convention of concealed emotion to ratify its own evident incapacity to handle genuine feeling at all. The tragedy of the death has to be left implied, unstated, reflected in objective consequences such as Brenda's desertion of Tony rather than in subjective response. We are meant to sense, throughout the event, a sort of significant emotional blankness: but 'blankness', as a term, runs together too indiscriminately stunned trauma on the one hand and shallow indifference on the other. At the point of explicit feeling, Waugh withdraws quickly to the style of the early satires:

> She wept helplessly, turning round in the chair and pressing her forehead against its gilt back.

Upstairs Mrs Northcote had Souki Foucauld-Esterhazy by
the foot and was saying, 'There are four men dominating your
fate. One is loyal and tender but has not yet disclosed his
love. . . .'

John Andrew's death brings home to Brenda her love for
Beaver: she believes at first that it is Beaver who has been
killed, and 'Until (then), when I thought something had happened to you, I had no idea that I loved you'. To this extent
John Andrew's sudden death (he is kicked in the head by a
horse) has some plot-relevance, as it has also in being responsible
for the final sundering of Brenda and Tony. Yet the incident,
nevertheless, seems too dramatic for its functional role within
the narrative: its literal and metaphorical meanings seem
curiously disjunctive. On any realistic estimate, it would hardly
take the news of Beaver's supposed death to convince Brenda
of a passionate love for him—although the fact that an artificial
and extraordinary crisis of this kind is needed to shift the level
of the relationship from casual encounter to 'love' has its own
significance. The whole incident is unconvincing: and in any
case it imbues John Andrew's death with narrative-significance
only by a very circuitous route. Again, John Andrew never
seemed sufficiently important to either of his parents to prevent
a divorce if it had been really wanted; so in this sense, too, the
death, viewed realistically, is less than plausible. The fact is
that John Andrew's death, given its seriousness, is nevertheless
more than a little reminiscent of the passing of Lord Tangent
and similar grotesque accidents in the earlier novels. Like those
incidents it is imposed on the novel, as a random, shocking,
gratuitous gesture to the brutal absurdity of life, a testimony to
the impossibility of order and control. The death is a stupid
accident which 'just happened', which is 'nobody's fault': to
this extent it acts as an effective image of the upper-class world,
which is similarly brutal and absurd but whose aberrations 'just
happen', without too-specific moral blame. The whole incident,
like Flossie's dramatic death-fall from a chandelier in *Vile
Bodies*, hints at an underlying, violent negativity which it is

unable formally to articulate or account for; as such, it is again less a 'profound' image than a symptom of helpless disturbance. One is forced to conclude from the book as a whole that Waugh does not know how serious he is intending to be, as the frequent lapses into a *Vile Bodies* brand of satirical whimsy sufficiently evidence. The whole episode of Tony's divorce-proceedings—the overnight stay in a Brighton hotel, the attendant detectives—is another case in point: the fact that the divorce merely involves Tony in going through certain ridiculous, external motions is offered as an image of the grotesque, game-like quality of life; but it is also (as the satirical indulgence of these scenes indicates) the kind of behaviour which Waugh is happiest with, the nearest he can come to significant feeling.

The latter part of *A Handful of Dust* is devoted to Tony's adventures in South America, and his fateful encounter with the sinister Mr Todd. There are, of course, certain thematic congruencies between this part of the novel and what has gone before: in both cases, Tony is the victim of predatory forces, so that the macabre ritual of reading Dickens in the jungle is intended to parallel the futile round of English upper-class life. Both are mockeries of civilised culture, set in the midst of an encroaching chaos. Despite this thematic parallel, however, the two parts of the novel really fail to cohere: and they fail primarily because the South American experience is uncertainly handled. As a total episode, the wanderings in Pie-wie country are too realistically detailed, in the close physical descriptions of landscape and event, to be of merely 'symbolic' importance; yet that, finally, is their upshot, when Tony stumbles on Mr Todd at the heart of darkness. It is not difficult to see that this ambivalence results from the novel's mixed intentions, in translating Tony from his ancestral seat to the tropics. On the one hand, the South American venture is a contact with 'real' experience—with hardship, sickness, physical exertion, a vividly present landscape—in contrast to the hermetic unrealities of fashionable London; but on the other hand it is the symbolic projection of Tony's hopeless search for the paradisal city of truth, and so an extension of the novel's pessimistic 'waste land' thesis. The two elements, of realism and fantasy, interweave constantly in Last's feverish consciousness.

If the episode is taken as 'realistic', it is too sharply disjointed from what went before and has no effective point of purchase on that English experience. This, indeed, is the dominant impression of the early descriptions of Tony's expedition, which involve an inexplicably abrupt transition from one level to another. But if it is taken as 'symbolic', it fits in with the English experience rather too neatly: it goes to 'prove', by the easy choice of a particular, realistically incredible metaphor, that the emptiness glimpsed at the core of a declining English culture is indeed universal and metaphysical. The whole episode, in other words, seems too realistic to justify its symbolic point, and too symbolic to justify its realism. Waugh wants to use foreign experience in two ways: as an escape from relative unreality to relative reality; and as an extended symbol of contemporary fever, chaos and futility. Yet these modes obviously conflict: and in the end the symbolic meaning predominates, to suggest that there is, after all, no escape to a reality beyond Society. The American exploration reveals the hollowness of English culture as 'metaphysically' rather than socially determined, and to this extent deepens a revolted sense of its vacuity; yet the subversiveness of that insight is curtailed by the fact that experience elsewhere is, by the same token, equally corrupt. It is a 'human' rather than a social condition which is flawed; and this, while it intensifies the *significance* of English social decline, also removes its precise causes beyond the social arena. The victimisation of Tony is finally the work, not just of identifiable and changeable social factors (the fickle exploitations of a decadent social class, epitomised in Brenda), but of the 'human condition' itself, which appears indifferently in Brenda Last and Mr Todd.

Waugh's choice of South America as the locus of a non-English reality deserves a final comment. English experience, in the light of Tony Last's sufferings, appears cheap and devaluated; but it is interesting that the only alternative form of life is one notable for the extremity of its difference from England. There is, in other words, no way of exposing the decadence of fashionable London from within the society itself—no other range of English social value or experience to which an appeal can be made. The upper class may be corrupt, but its complacent belief that it *is* England is accepted at face-value; and then there is nowhere to go but half-way across the world. Because *that* environment is alien and sinister, wholly different from England, it can act as an index of the extremity with which England has been rejected; yet for the same reasons, it cannot act as an effective critical standpoint on the society which has been abandoned. It is simply another world, and no fruitful commerce (other than at the level of generalising metaphor) can be established between it and home. Like the white slave traffic of *Decline and Fall* (which was also, significantly, connected with Latin America), the realms of action and experience which might supply material for a criticism of England are so extreme as to be fantastically unreal. Whether, then, South America is seen 'realistically' or 'symbolically', it can furnish no genuine point of transcendence for those Englishmen weary of their own class. Viewed realistically, it is too alien to be effective; viewed symbolically, it is merely an intensified projection (for both Tony Last and, in *Brideshead Revisited*, Charles Ryder, who also spends some time there) of the blankness discerned at home.

Brideshead Revisited seems to me superior to the other novels we have discussed; and it is interesting to see that, despite the sourness and snobbery of his special pleading for the aristocratic order (the vulgar gibes at 'humane legislation' and the rest), Waugh is at his best as a writer when the anaesthetised neutrality of the earlier satire gives way to a form of fiction in which his own feelings are directly engaged. *Brideshead Revisited* is a successful novel; but it does not escape from the ambiguities we have examined already, in relation to Waugh's simultaneous criticism and defence of the upper class. In this novel, that ambiguity assumes two general forms: one concerns the conflict between 'morality' and 'style'; the other relates to the characterisation of Sebastian Flyte.

On a superficial reading, *Brideshead* is a puzzling novel to interpret. Its general intention, evident enough throughout the book but also explicitly announced by its author in his 1959 Preface, is to make out a defence of the social order which the Marchmains of Brideshead symbolise, in face of the vulgarity and commercialism which are undermining it. Parts of the book—in particular the Prologue, Epilogue, and much of Book 3—would seem to bear out this purpose. In the Prologue and Epilogue, the Brideshead tradition is seen as subject to external assault from a new philistinism; in Book 3, Charles Ryder and Julia Marchmain are portrayed as the shipwrecked victims of a distasteful civilisation, clinging to each other in a storm of social disintegration which they see as 'a conspiracy against us'. Yet it is obvious enough, elsewhere in the novel, that responsibility for the Marchmain decline lies, not with conspiring invasions from the outside, but with the Marchmains themselves. Lord Marchmain has relinquished his traditional duties in England for a life of pleasure in Europe; Sebastian squanders his life in drink; Brideshead, the elder son, devotes his time to collecting matchboxes; and Julia, like Charles Ryder, makes an unhappy marriage for unadmirably ambitious motives. Both Julia and Brideshead marry representatives of the 'vulgar' middle class, and to this extent the tradition disintegrates under a combination of 'internal' and 'external' pressures; but both choose their partners consciously, and are in no sense passively enticed. The house of Brideshead is on the wane, as Rex Mottram crudely but correctly puts it, because of its own wasteful prodigality; the process, essentially, is one of self-destruction.

None of this is ignored by the novel; but it is surrounded by an interesting ambivalence of feeling, which relates to the conflict between 'morality' and 'style'. The plain fact is that, with the exception of the younger daughter Cordelia and (with some qualifications to be made later) Lady Marchmain, none of the family is especially admirable from the viewpoint of the traditional moral order it is supposed to sustain. Yet it is this unpromising material which must somehow be wrought into an impassioned defence of traditional upper-class England. In one sense, the problem dissolves because these moral discriminations are unimportant: it is the 'mood' rather than the precise character of the Marchmain family which seduces Charles Ryder, and that mood survives the recognition of particular moral foibles. The episode when Charles is upbraided by Lady Marchmain for giving Sebastian money for drink is a case in point:

> I was unmoved; there was no part of me remotely touched by her distress. It was as I had often imagined being expelled from school. I almost expected to hear her say: 'I have already written to inform your unhappy father'. But as I drove away and turned back in the car to take what promised to be my last view of the house, I felt that I was leaving part of myself behind, and that wherever I went afterwards I should feel the lack of it. . . . A door had shut, the low door in the wall I had sought and found in Oxford; open it now and I should find no enchanted garden.

Ryder detects the falsely sermonising tone in Lady Marchmain's rebuke, but it is not enough to bring about disenchantment; in this respect, as in others, the novel maintains that characteristic English upper-class commitment to 'place' and 'family' which can seem curiously independent of the precise qualities of particular people.

There is, nevertheless, a problem in justifying the particular qualities of the Marchmains, if the case for aristocratic England is to appear convincing. Lady Marchmain remains admirable in Ryder's eyes because style overrides morality; and this is also true in the cases of Lord Marchmain and Sebastian. Both men have their 'fling', and in doing so desert the old faith; but the fling, with its brio and panache, is at once morally problematic and a revelation of what the novel applauds most in the blood of the gentry. The general attitude to Sebastian and his father is therefore ambiguous: both must finally be brought low, but both are indulged in the process.

In Charles's early days at Oxford, his cousin Jasper fills the role of Potts in *Decline and Fall*: the earnest, industrious man of integrity who shows up as deadly dull when measured against the whimsical charm of Sebastian. On the other hand, Sebastian has a latent 'seriousness' (how convincing a seriousness we shall examine later) which saves him from the uncertain moral censure reserved for Anthony Blanche, whose flamboyant decadence is sinisterly complete. Blanche, of course, is 'outrageously' amusing and in some ways admired, but Charles is significantly hesitant in his attitude towards him, 'enjoying him voraciously' one minute, disliking him the next. Blanche represents the Sebastian style carried to a tainted and parodic extreme, and so is attractive in his resemblance to Sebastian but distasteful in so far as he displays the admired upper-class manner in its worst light, shorn of its saving moral strengths. (He is, of course, modelled on Brian Howard; but it is interesting that Waugh has also made him a *déraciné* Jewish nomad of obscure nationality. It is his lack of 'place' and 'family' which allow him finally to be dismissed, as a foreign, un-English deviation from the Marchmain norm.) Sebastian, then, stands midway between the despised 'morality' of cousin Jasper and the prancing eccentricities of the alien Blanche, although leaning unmistakably in the latter direction; he is a fashionable wastrel, coyly devoted to his large teddy bear, but has flashes of a 'deeper' self.

In this sense, Sebastian's decadence is not allowed to count too heavily against him. In its early, Oxford stages, it emerges as an attractive panache; in its later, dipsomaniac developments, it assumes a tragic quality which lends him 'serious' status. Sebastian's final return to his Catholic faith, as a burnt-out drifter in Morocco, is in one way an expiation: 'style' must be progressively eroded to nothing for true sanctity to appear. Yet it also goes to signify the latent resources of true aristocracy: like his father and Julia, Sebastian is able finally to confront and embrace the spiritual reality from which he has strayed. The decline of Sebastian, Lord Marchmain and Julia is thus a criticism of irresponsible aristocracy, but also a testing-ground of its superior strength: all three display, at the point of seemingly irreparable breakdown, the workings of a subconscious grace which, in so far as it is an aspect of their social lineage, underlines the superior virtue of that tradition even where it seems most corrupted. The sanctification of Sebastian, the death-bed repentance of Lord Marchmain and the renewal of Julia's faith are 'twitches upon the thread' which binds and recalls them to their spiritual centre no matter how far they wander.

It is important, however, to question the precise application of this metaphor, which Waugh takes as the title of his third part. What it suggests is an ultimate (although strictly qualified) victory which is in some sense inevitable. The Catholic aristocrat will have his fling, so enacting the attractively 'Byronic' features of his character, but it will not, in the end, count too heavily against him: he will return at last to spiritual base, so proving the impressively 'moral' fibre of his deeper identity. It is a version of Augustine's 'Oh God, make me good but not yet': and indeed that phrase is actually quoted by Sebastian. And because what motivates the return to base is the action of grace, which is closed to ordinary analysis, there is no way of arguing against this thesis on its own terms. Where it seems most vulnerable, however, is in its unavoidable appearance of having things both ways: of fulfilling style and morality at once. For it is these dimensions which the book, like other of Waugh's novels, finds most difficult to reconcile. Cordelia Marchmain, who takes up social work in Spain, is the most spiritually devout of her family; yet Ryder's sensibility is wounded by her total lack of style:

> It hurt to think of Cordelia growing up 'quite plain', to think of all that burning love spending itself on serum-injections and de-lousing powder. When she arrived, tired from her journey, rather shabby, moving in the manner of one who had no interest in pleasing, I thought her an ugly woman. . . . She

was . . . without any of Julia's or Sebastian's grace, without Brideshead's gravity. She seemed brisk and matter-of-fact, steeped in the atmosphere of camp and dressing-station, so accustomed to gross suffering as to lose the finer shades of pleasure.

Brideshead is similarly ungracious: a placid, inert, ponderously monastic figure:

> . . . he was usually preposterous yet somehow achieved a certain dignity by his remoteness and agelessness; he was still half-child, already half-veteran; there seemed no spark of contemporary life in him; he had a kind of massive rectitude and impermeability, an indifference to the world, which compelled respect. Though we often laughed at him, he was never wholly ridiculous; at times he was even formidable.

Both Brideshead and Cordelia are admired for their integrity, but grudgingly: the moral heritage of aristocracy, the dutifully responsible conscience, is preserved intact in them both, but only at the expense of Sebastian's mannered vivacity. Waugh does not actually go so far as to regret Cordelia's *wasting* of her love on human caring, for this would be to tip the balance too decisively on the side of style; but the implication behind the semi-neutral verb 'spending' is clear enough. The novel's feelings are thus deeply ambiguous: sanctity can emerge only through the purgation of an irresponsible frivolity, a suffering encounter with reality; yet the brief years in the enchanted garden are nostalgically mourned. That world is recognised as unreal—it is compared to a conjurer's delusive apparatus—yet it cannot be disengaged from; and its inherent self-destructiveness can still be conveniently glossed over for the purposes of a propagandist tirade against the 'Hoopers', symbols of the new vulgarity:

> These men must die to make a world for Hooper; they were the aborigines, vermin by right of law, to be shot off at leisure so that things might be safe for the travelling salesman, with his polygonal pince-nez, his fat wet handshake, his grinning dentures. I wondered, as the train carried me further and further

from Lady Marchmain, whether perhaps there was not on her, too, the same blaze, marking her and hers for destruction by other ways than war.

The final image is significantly falsifying, of a piece with the dyspeptic malice of the salesman caricature. It suggests, within the qualifying form of an idle musing, that the forms of destruction actually recorded in the novel—dipsomania, disease, financial extravagance, social ambition, old age, moral insensitivity —are neither neutrally biological nor humanly culpable, but amount instead, at some conveniently submerged 'spiritual' level, to an altruistic self-sacrifice for the benefit of the lower orders. Once more, positive value is salvaged from the facts of aristocratic decline in a way which seems no more than a crude opportunism. We are expected to forget that Brideshead is declining, among other reasons, because its bank-account is overdrawn by one hundred thousand pounds: for this criticism is put into the mouth of Rex Mottram, the vulgar Canadian *nouveau riche* with no taste for Burgundy, and so made to seem a symptom of his own venality rather than a statement of fact.

The ambiguity of the novel's attitude to the causes of the Brideshead decline relates to its treatment of Sebastian. The chief reason for Sebastian's alcoholism is his family: this much is explicitly stated more than once, but what it means is rather less evident. The difficulty lies in the fact that we are never given sufficient evidence either to verify or adequately disprove the suggestion that it is the Marchmains who drive Sebastian to drink; what evidence we have is obscure, fragmentary and conflicting, given in mysterious intimations rather than directly:

> He leaned forward and put the car into gear. 'It's where my family live'; and even then, rapt in the vision, I felt, momentarily, an ominous chill at the words he used—not, 'that is my house', but 'it's where my family live'. . . .
>
> The further we drove from Brideshead, the more he seemed to cast off his uneasiness—the almost furtive restlessness and irritability that had possessed him. . . .

Now Sebastian had withdrawn into that other life of his
where I was not asked to follow, and I was left, instead, forlorn
and regretful. . . .

That night I began to realise how little I really knew of
Sebastian, and to understand why he had always sought to keep
me apart from the rest of his life. . . .

'Ominous chill', 'furtive restlessness', 'that other life': the whole
relation between Sebastian and his family is shrouded in this
faintly melodramatic language, tantalisingly opaque and impenetrable. The question is whether what is at work here is
a mystery or a mystification: whether there are identifiable
reasons, behind the veil of secrecy, for this furtiveness, or
whether what we have is essentially a set of 'ominous' gestures
with little substantial behind them. Returning these passages
to the whole context of the novel, one is forced to conclude that
the 'mystery' is less an objective reality than a device on the
novel's part for obscuring essential evidence. The key-figure in
the 'persecution' of Sebastian is his mother, Lady Marchmain;
and if it were possible to define a coherent attitude towards
her, it would also be possible to determine the objective validity
of Sebastian's sense of victimisation. But the presentation of
Lady Marchmain is in fact thoroughly ambiguous. Anthony
Blanche sees her as a vampire, placing the blame for Lord
Marchmain's desertion firmly on her shoulders; but Blanche
is engaged in a spiteful campaign to turn Charles against the
Marchmains, and his testimony is therefore of limited value.
(He is, however, notably perceptive in other matters—in his
judgement of Charles's artistic abilities, for instance—and to
this extent is not easily dismissable.) Cara, Lord Marchmain's
mistress, sees Lady Marchmain as 'a good and simple woman';
but she also tells Charles that both Sebastian and his father
detest Lady Marchmain, with a loathing deep enough to suggest, perhaps, a genuine cause. Charles himself is grateful for
Lady Marchmain's 'abundant kindness' to him; but he is also
sharply conscious of the calculating, possessive mind at work
beneath the deceptive smoothness of her charm. That feeling,

in turn, is checked by a sense of her suffering 'saintliness':
Cordelia, whose moral judgement is to be trusted, believes
firmly in her mother's sanctity. So it is a matter of accommodating Cordelia's statement to the petty falsities and possessive
tactics of which Ryder is himself aware, and which are supposed to be a motivating factor in Sebastian's escape into
alcoholism.

The function of the 'mystery' surrounding Sebastian's relations with his family is really to evade the difficulties of this
accommodation. Either Sebastian's growing alcoholism has
intelligible causes rooted in his family context, in which case
the Marchmains are open to some particularly damaging criticism; or it has not, in which case the blame shifts either to
Sebastian himself or to some kind of inherited Ibsenite disorder
in the blood. The problem is that the novel really wants to
avoid all these solutions at once. To suggest that the Marchmain
family has literally reduced its younger son to a burnt-out
alcoholic wreck would interfere somewhat with that nostalgic
apologia for English ancestral seats which it is *Brideshead*'s
declared purpose to launch; to suggest that Sebastian's collapse
is his own fault would badly harm the idyllic vision of
indolent drinking days in Oxford. Sebastian, not Charles,
is, after all, the novel's hero, and it would hardly do to
imply that he was simply a self-indulgent profligate. The only
remaining answer is that Sebastian is gripped by a disease
in the blood, by the traditional aristocratic death-wish: and
this, indeed, is explicitly said by Cara, who draws attention
to the evident similarity between Sebastian's escapism and
the flight of his father. 'Alex was nearly a drunkard when he
met me; it is in the blood.' But the novel will not have this
either:

Julia used to say, 'Poor Sebastian. It's something chemical in
him.'
That was the cant phrase of the time, derived from heaven
knows what misconception of popular science. 'There's something chemical between them' was used to explain the over-

mastering hate or love of any two people. It was the old concept
of determinism in a new form. I do not believe there was anything chemical in my friend.

The bristling, slightly priggish quality of this reflects a traditionally genteel distaste for 'science', as well as a patrician contempt
for 'environmental' or psychological accounts of human behaviour. The same attitude is taken, later in the novel, towards
the admission of Sebastian to a psychiatric clinic, which is pro-
posed, significantly, by Rex Mottram and opposed by Ryder
and Cordelia. So if Sebastian's troubles are to be explained
neither by environment, psychology or culpable free action,
they must be 'spiritually' motivated; but in that case it is difficult to understand the emphasis laid by both the novel and
Sebastian himself on the Marchmain family as the reason for
his decline. That emphasis is strong enough to intimate a kind
of reason, and so to give Sebastian's career some realistic credi-
bility; but it cannot be too fully explicated, for that would be
to expose the family to a damning charge. Because of these
confusions, the general *impression* given by Sebastian's fall is
that of a tragic symbol of aristocratic decline in the world
of the Hoopers and Mottrams: the death of grace and charm.
This thesis, which like Ryder's musings on the blaze of destruction set on the Marchmains, implies that the tradition is being
externally rather than internally eroded, will not bear too close
an examination: but from a distance, given the confusions of
realistic motivation, it can stand.

Sebastian's fall is, of course, closely bound up with his
Catholicism and the religious pressures of his family, and it is
worth adding a final comment on this. The main effect of the
Marchmains' religion, in Charles's eyes, is to deepen his sense
of their mystery: Sebastian's faith is an 'enigma' to him, an
inscrutable but obscurely attractive dimension which is lacking
in himself. But it is difficult, again, not to feel that the 'mystery'
is rather too easily come by—asserted rather than substantiated.
There is this reflection of Ryder's on a casual comment by
Brideshead, for instance:

'You can't stop people if they want to get drunk. My mother couldn't stop my father, you know.'

He spoke in his odd, impersonal way. The more I saw of this family, I reflected, the more singular I found them.

What is really singular is that Ryder should interpret a perfectly ordinary remark as evidence of some profoundly impenetrable riddle in the quality of the family's life. What we *see* of their religious faith, early in the novel, amounts to little more than Cordelia's childhood chatter about novenas and Brideshead's pedantic scholasticism; yet Charles is ready, even at this point, to take these trivialities as symptomatic of some deeper experience. In Sebastian himself, that deeper experience, like the question of his relation to his family, can be hinted at but not shown, for style and morality do not mix:

> 'Oh dear, it's very difficult being a Catholic.'
> 'Does it make much difference to you?'
> 'Of course. All the time.'
> 'Well, I can't say I've noticed it. . . .'

We are expected to believe Sebastian's assertion (retrospectively, at least), but also to take the point of Charles's caustic rejoinder: it is important that Sebastian's spirituality should be sufficiently suggested for his final return to the Church to appear natural, but sufficiently concealed not to interfere with his style. Once more, the sense of mystery is really a device: it is partly a way of gratuitously 'glamourising' the Marchmains, partly a way of hinting at a level of experience which cannot be directly articulated because to do so would be to run the risk of a dull, Brideshead-like moral earnestness. The problem which the novel faces, given its distaste for theological argument and practical works of mercy, is to redeem Sebastian without landing him in the camp of Brideshead, or even of Cordelia. It is for this reason that the Sebastian we see is religious only in a 'subliminal' sense, and the saint he develops into is a man we do not see, living in a country beyond England and the limits of the novel.

III

The conflict of style and morality in *Brideshead Revisited*, and the uncertainty which surrounds Sebastian, are aspects of a more persistent ambivalence which we have seen in other of Waugh's novels: the need to defend, at certain crucial points, an English upper-class world which is also satirised. In this respect, for all his specific differences of treatment and subject-matter, Waugh offers an important parallel to Woolf, Forster and Huxley. Upper-class values are false, devious and dangerously hermetic, in the earlier satiric novels; and a sense of their partial, fragmentary nature can move quickly into 'panic and emptiness', the vertiginous nausea which Nina feels in the last scene of *Vile Bodies*. But though these values are partial and unreal, they are also, paradoxically, all there is: there can be no effective appeal beyond them to a wider social experience, for the values survive only by virtue of their exclusiveness. The break for reality, as in the Leonard Bast episodes of *Howard's End*, results only in failure and frustration.

There is a relation between the quality of upper-class values in Waugh and the literary techniques of his novels. What gives those values their taint of unreality is their distance from the pressures of social necessity: from the constrictions of a settled, permanent, complex and institutionalised social fabric, of the sort that Nina glimpses from the aeroplane. Because upper-class experience is damagingly free of these shaping restrictions, it moves easily into fantasy, and then into nightmare; because this privileged life-style is independent of necessity, the experience it generates may be permutated, manipulated and combined, without the restraining intervention of fact. Waugh's satirical novels offer a vivid kaleidoscope in which any fragment of experience can be made to merge into any other, in which any pattern may be randomly produced by a shake or tilt of the focus. They are areas of pure freedom in which anything can happen, for there are no pre-established necessities;

yet that freedom is the negative liberation of fantasy, liable at any moment to disintegrate under the anxiety of its own giddy unconstraint. Because all is possible to this privileged social class and to the literary form which mirrors it, nothing is especially valuable; because no convention or definition is more than improvised, momentary, experimental, no event or identity can be given the fixed limits of substantial meaning. It is a world close to that of Huxley's early novels, in which ideas, fantasies, insights and hypotheses can be shuttled, crossed and combined in rapid, 'brilliant' succession because none of them is in the least subject to the constraints of social reality.

It is in this respect, as we shall see in the following chapter, that the English upper-class novel differs most from its lower middle-class counterpart. Whereas the lower middle-class novel remains, on the whole, passively imprisoned within the texture of 'ordinary' life, able to imagine but not to enact ways of transcending this seedy, quotidian realm, the upper-class novel is fixed at a point of anxious estrangement from the routine fabric of social experience. That estrangement is at once the root of its nausea and the obstacle to its cure: for the version of the ordinary world to which it gives rise—the view of suburbia from the aeroplane—is an ugly and distasteful one, which must be rejected. It is in this sense that the upper-class novel, while at one point, as we have seen, diametrically opposed to its lower middle-class counterpart, is also a parallel case. Both *genres* are acutely aware of the impoverishment of their own typical experience; but neither is in the end capable of rising above that fragmentary living to grasp a more 'total' and 'objective' version of its society. Such a version was possible to the major tradition of nineteenth-century realism, and was a primary source of its achievement: in that *genre*, the partial perceptions of a specific social class or group could be 'placed' within the complex orchestrations of a unified vision. In the twentieth century, that unity is decisively ruptured. Both the upper-class and lower middle-class novels confront panic and emptiness, as an 'objective' quality of contemporary experience; yet that sense of uncontrolled collapse is, equally, the quality of a constricted social vision in the novel itself, unable to pass beyond its own specialised social experience to discern and evaluate the total structure of which it is a part.

CHAPTER III

George Orwell and the Lower Middle-class Novel

I

W E are used to distinguishing kinds of novel by literary *genre* rather than by social class, and the argument of this chapter is not particularly to question the first mode of discrimination in the name of the second. There is little to be gained by a crude reduction of novels to the ranges of social experience with which they deal; but there is, perhaps, some point in recognising that particular *genres* of novel seem intimately related to particular areas of social reality. This seems especially true of the *genre* we loosely term 'naturalism': the novel which aims to achieve a frank, detailed and faithful exposure of social experience, and in particular of kinds of social experience which are by conventional standards 'vulgar' or drably quotidian.

In its major European formulations, naturalism was concerned with the shocking and radical impact of these concealed realms of social existence on what it viewed as a hypocritical social and aesthetic code; it aimed to be both sensationally unorthodox and grimly veracious. Yet conscious unorthodoxy is not, on the whole, the aspect of the movement which emerged in English literature. As a phase of critical philosophy and aesthetics, naturalism hardly existed in England as it did in Europe; and a consequence of this is that the naturalistic 'tradition' in England is less a subversive revelation of submerged social realities than a form of explicit 'social realism' with a radical tinge. If we look at the naturalistic novel in the last decades of the nineteenth century—at Gissing, Moore, Mark Rutherford, Arthur Morrison—then at Bennett and Wells, and onward to Orwell and the social realism of the

1930s, we can see no simple diagram. Gissing's middle-class 'radicalism', Moore's confused career of symbolism and aestheticism, Wells's developments of Fabianism, Bennett's interest in scientific evolutionary doctrines, Orwell's socialism: these are 'radical' interests of a kind, but, with the exception of Wells, none of these writers achieved anything like that systematic critique of their society which was integral to the naturalist movement in Europe. What these novelists do have in common, in fact, is their ambivalent relationship to the social experience they dramatise. They are all concerned to expose an oppressiveness, anxiety and deprivation which is to them a determining truth of the society and yet which does not get into its conventional literary art; yet although 'radical' in this sense, in relation to literary orthodoxies and upper-class manners, their critique of a conservative society remains for the most part unformulated and inarticulate.

It is at this point that the class-bearings of English naturalism are significant. The ethos of English naturalism, from Gissing and Bennett to Wells and Orwell, is distinctively lower middle class. The English naturalist novel, in its main tendencies, emerges at a point of vulnerable insecurity within the lower middle class, wedged painfully between the working class on the one hand and the dominant social class on the other, but unable to identify itself with either. It is the world of the struggling journalist, the draper's assistant, the provincial shopkeeper or manufacturer, the small hotel proprietor, the petty colonial official, the suburban insurance clerk. It reaches its epitome, in the literature of the twentieth century, in the shrewd but seedy figure of Leopold Bloom. It is a world intelligent enough to feel acutely the meanness of its own typical experience, but powerless to transcend it; a world suspicious alike of the sophisticated manners of its rulers and the uncouthness of its working-class inferiors. It knows its own life to be trivialised and demeaning, and struggles to maintain decencies and pretensions which define more sharply that precariously thin line which divides it from the 'lower' classes; yet it values the solid realism and practicality of its own behaviour against the rarefied unrealities of the class above it. As such, it is 'radical' and 'conservative' at once: too crushingly aware of the cheapness of its own experience to be fulfilled, yet too deeply in debt to the established society to countenance the bolshevism of its inferiors or the ideological talk of dandyish intellectuals. It despises the upper middle class, yet clings to it as the horizon of its own ambition.

The consequence of this ambiguity is a peculiar tension within the lower middle-class novel, which we shall examine in some detail in the case of George Orwell.[1] In most of these novels, the quality of common life is seen as radically impoverished: the world, in the pregnant words of Wells's Mr Polly, is a 'beastly silly wheeze of a Hole', thwarting, sterile and deadeningly repressive. Yet precisely because this existence, despite its seediness, is 'real', in contrast to the inane frivolities of the socially successful or the impenetrable lives of the genuinely poor (who are hardly human at all), there is nowhere else to turn. And because of this, the 'reality' can be transmuted into a kind of virtue. There can be breaks to a pastoral dream beyond society (successful in Mr Polly's case, disastrous in the case of Orwell's George Bowling), a flight to foreign worlds (Bennett's Sophie Baines), an interim entry into the life of the rich (Kipps) or the very poor (Gordon Comstock); but these alternatives, apart from the improbable case of Polly, are really deceptive: modes of escape or moral gestures which the inescapable lower middle-class realities will expose as false. For the naturalist novelist, men are capable of a limited transcendence of their determining environments—they can, if they are sufficiently sensitive, identify and fight its sterility—but it is part of the philosophical assumptions of naturalism, which the English novel (and Bennett in particular) inherits, that men are

[1] Orwell himself, of course, was not lower middle class in origin: he was born into an equally insecure stratum at the lower end of the upper class, but transplanted those tensions into what emerges, in some of his novels, as a definitively lower middle-class ethos.

passively bound to their situations by only partially controllable forces. It is this philosophical attitude which intersects, in the history of naturalism, with the structure of feeling of a particular class, able to reflect on its own misery but unable, precisely because of the pressing fact of that misery, to conceive of an alternative. If it is broadly true of the upper middle-class novel that it can imagine organisations of value and idea only on account of its privileged isolation from the pressures of social necessity, the same is true of its lower middle-class counterpart: it can escape from urgent social pressures only at the cost of abstraction or deception.

Arnold Bennett's *The Old Wives' Tale* interestingly illustrates some of these general attitudes. The young Sophie Baines is the object of some gentle satire for her desire to escape the stifling limits of the Five Towns; yet it is also true that what she feels of its restrictive puritanism and pretence is substantially borne out by the novel's own viewpoint. The book uses Sophie's experience in Paris, most evidently on her return to England, as a way of focusing the cheapness and rigidity of Bursley life; yet at the same time it appeals to Bursley values in order to condemn Sophie's 'sin' in deserting the provincial world for a cosmopolitan rake. Gerald Scales, the rake in question, is criticised by the standard of those values—'the accumulated strength of generations of honest living'—even though what we have seen of that 'honest living' is largely a complex set of narrowly self-righteous deceptions and philistine pretentiousness. Bennett's laboriously heavy-handed satire of the Bursley world, his pedantically exact clinicism of analysis, is intended to reveal its weaknesses; but it is obvious how closely that stylistic mode, with its irrelevant detailing of items of furniture and pseudo-scientific circumlocutions, is in fact bound to the world it is supposed to be 'placing'. The Bursley characters are described as 'organisms', in the dehumanising terms common to a naturalist tradition which Orwell inherited; yet when it is a matter of repelling the claims of an alternative order of life—the decadent lure of Paris, the attitudes of 'emancipated' Englishmen or loose-living foreigners—Bursley be-comes, quite suddenly, a resource of 'honest living'. Its values can finally triumph over the dangerously foreign: Sophie runs a Parisian boarding-house with all the puritan canniness of her Staffordshire ancestors.

Bennett, then, for all his careful stance of scientific neutrality, is able to endorse the merit of the Bursley world. It is inade-quate, but it is better than most alternatives; Sophie's frustra-tion elicits a kind of sympathy, but her break to transcend an environment can only end in hubristic death. There is a parallel, but also significantly different process at work in Wells's *The History of Mr Polly*. At the beginning of the novel, Polly's forlorn cry of '*Beastly* Silly Wheeze of a Hole' is instantly followed by a reservation:

> He suffered from indigestion now nearly every afternoon, but as he lacked introspection he projected the associated discomfort upon the world. . . . Mr Polly sat on the stile and hated the whole scheme of life—which was at once excessive and inade-quate of him.

Polly's disgusted response to his social situation has, as the novel will show, objective grounds; yet at the same time the lower middle-class hero must not be allowed the introspection to analyse his own condition, for it is precisely that lack of ability to 'totalise', and so actively transcend, his situation which lies at the heart of his problem. He is intelligent enough to re-act correctly, but not to perceive the whole condition of which, for his author, he is merely an interesting symptom. The in-digestion is thus the novel's device for detaching itself from any full identification with Polly's helplessly reflex reaction, while at the same time sympathising (from a more intelligently analytical viewpoint) with his response. (We shall see some-thing of the same device in Orwell's treatment of Gordon Comstock in *Keep the Aspidistra Flying*.) Polly has a dim dis-cernment that there is more to the scheme of life than 'things that are jolly and "bits of all right" ', but it is an insight which lurks 'deep in his being', too fragmentary for direct articulation.

He is, in other words, the archetypal lower middle-class hero, obscurely conscious of a pervasive disintegration which is too closely interwoven in his personal experience to be formulated into anything resembling a 'position'. Where the novel differs most from *The Old Wives' Tale*, of course, is in Polly's ability to walk away from the detested *petit bourgeois* world; yet the escape, with its images of arson and arcadia, is really a movement of fantasy, which abandons rather than changes the world.

What is remarkable about Wells, of all the English naturalistic novelists, is that he himself developed a highly formulated 'totalisation' of the social breakdown from which Polly suffers —one which transcended the confused fragments of immediate experience, and provided a framework within which its historical significance could be judged. But such an organisation was, by definition, denied to characters such as Polly, and so created a difficulty. The problem was to bring that explanatory framework to bear on the detail of raw experience: to connect the quality of that experience, without falsification, to a total analysis which would render it structurally intelligible. And this seemed impossibly difficult to do. The problem becomes explicit in chapter seven of *Polly*, after Wells has quoted at length a sociological analysis of the condition of the lower middle class:

> I come back to Mr Polly, sitting upon his gate and swearing in the east wind, and so returning I have a sense of floating across unbridged abysses between the general and the particular. There, on the one hand, is the man of understanding seeing clearly—I suppose he sees clearly—the big process that dooms millions of lives to thwarting and discomfort and unhappy circumstances, and giving us no help, no hint, by which we may get that better 'collective will and intelligence' which would dam that stream of human failure; and on the other hand, Mr Polly, sitting on his gate, untrained, unwarned, confused, distressed, angry, seeing nothing except that he is, as it were, netted in greyness and discomfort. . . .

It is, to recall a parallel case, the problem of Kipps, whose response to socialism is to admit that 'I can't argue about it, but it doesn't seem real like to me'. 'Real' is the crucial term: for the naturalistic novel, as we shall see most acutely in the case of Orwell, theory and experience, living and understanding, fragmentary feeling and overall structure, are desperately difficult to connect. It is this which accounts for the principle of non-selectiveness at the root of the naturalist aesthetic. Wells's own difficulties certainly owe a good deal to the peculiarly abstract and intransigent quality of his 'totalisations': it is hardly surprising that the rift between Mr Polly's obscure disaffection and Wells's neat schemes of efficiently global centralisation looms improbably large. But the problem persists, despite these local causes, throughout this *genre* of novel: an impatient, distressed or disgusted rejection of contemporary social experience which at the same time refuses any total understanding, and so any alternative position, as abstract, morally pretentious, naïvely Romantic or 'ideological'. The provincial, puritan, lower middle-class world is hateful, but its pressures prevent any disengagement; and because puritan values are to that extent inescapable, any stance outside this world is condemned by them as an idle luxury. The limits of ordinary experience are too crippling to permit the kind of transcendence which might subject a whole social condition to principled criticism; and when this is seen, there is nothing left but to retreat to a dogged, disillusioned affirmation of the quotidian. It is this problem which we can now examine in the work of George Orwell.

II

Mr Polly's opening words have their direct echo in the first comment of Flory, hero of Orwell's early novel *Burmese Days*: ' "Bloody, bloody hole", he thought, looking down the hill'. Flory, the cynical but in some ways sensitive colonial timber-merchant, behaves humanely to the Burmese people in a context of vicious racialism; but his compromised scepticism will not allow him to take a positive stand on his own hatred of imperialism. The result is a listless self-disgust, closely involved with guilt: 'Oh what a place, what people! What a civilisation is this of ours—this godless civilisation founded on whisky, *Blackwood's* and the "Bonzo" pictures! God have mercy on us, for all of us are part of it.' The 'we' and 'us' insert the essential qualifications to a principled and forthright moral rejection: Flory is unable to press his dislike of colonialist racialism through to complete condemnation because the superior sensitivity which makes him a better, gentler man than his fellow-colonialists also deepens his self-criticism to the point where he is unable to place credence in the value of his own responses.

Burmese Days is widely known as an assault upon Anglo-Burma, but what is less often remembered is its half-convinced apology, through the focus of the self-doubting Flory, for some of the regime's worst aspects. 'Besides, you could forgive the Europeans a great deal of their bitterness. Living and working among Orientals would try the temper of a saint. . . . The life of the Anglo-Indian officials is not all jam. In comfortless camps, in sweltering offices, in gloomy dakbungalows smelling of dust and earth-oil, they earn, perhaps, the right to be a little disagreeable.' 'A little disagreeable', in the light of the brutal white-supremacy complex shown in the novel, seems something of an understatement; its real function is not so much to suggest a judicious 'balance', but to half-ratify Flory's incapacity to formulate his own confused feelings into an explicit position, to validate his sense of impotent complicity with what he hates. (It is, significantly, the 'atmosphere' rather than the political realities of imperialism he detests, a fact which itself implies a less than complete attitude and understanding.)

Flory veers between a frustrated raging at his compatriots (a feeling which the novel suggests is excessive and unfair) and what amounts to a declared cynicism. Neither attitude is really adequate: the first is too suggestive of the sort of committed moral judgement which can be achieved only by detaching oneself from a world of which one is part; the second, if consistently manifested, would make Flory no better than his fellow-countrymen. So the realities of Anglo-Burma can be neither totally accepted nor totally denied. On the one hand, there is this, familiarly Orwellian outburst against the Deputy Commissioner:

> Nasty old bladder of lard! he thought, watching Mr Macgregor up the road. How his bottom did stick out in those tight khaki shorts. Like one of those beastly middle-aged scoutmasters, homosexuals almost to a man, that you see photographs of in the illustrated papers. Dressing himself up in those ridiculous clothes and exposing his pudgy, dimpled knees, because it is the pukka sahib thing to take exercise before breakfast—disgusting!

It is the tone of outraged Orwellian decency: the shudder of the 'normal' man, with his sober, puritan, self-conciously ordinary values, at 'pansy' eccentricity of any kind; the tone of the criticism of the intellectual socialists and 'Nancy poets' in *The Road to Wigan Pier*, replete with a tough, swaggering sense of self-righteous masculinity. It is not far removed from the kind of snobbish, physical disgust which characterises the racialist Ellis in *Burmese Days*, and its quality of *physical* repulsion is important: by virtue of it, an emotional rejection can be satisfied which does not press through, in other than a generalised sense, to an evaluation of the system which Macgregor symbolises. On the other hand, because the feeling is unfocused and uncontrolled, missing the structure for the fragment of physical detail, it can turn, as easily, against Flory himself, in a callous self-deprecation which 'realistically' undercuts the possibility of genuine criticism: 'Seditious?' Flory said. '*I'm* not seditious. I don't want the Burmans to drive us out of this country. God forbid! I'm here to make money, like everyone else. All I object to is the slimy white man's burden humbug. The pukka sahib pose. It's so boring.' This is intended to suggest a toughly attractive honesty—a rejection of colonial

pretence, and so, to that degree, a moral superiority to others—
at the same time as it binds Flory *to* those others, in his declared
corruption of motive. It accepts the burden of guilt in order
to avoid the contaminating risks of a moral stance—which
would, presumably, be just one more form of 'humbug'. Flory
must resist any suggestion that he is morally more sensitive
or altruistic than others (even though, as the novel will show
us, he clearly *is*) because this would be to take a stand on
principle which his collusion with colonialism denies him, and
so to live with the intolerable tension of bad faith. And so
'honesty' and 'pretence' are substituted, as moral alternatives,
for good and bad.

The true corruption of imperialism, in fact, is that it denies
the possibility of reliance on one's own 'good' feelings:

> You see louts fresh from school kicking grey-haired servants.
> And the time comes when you burn with hatred of your own
> countrymen, when you long for a native rising to drown their
> Empire in blood. And in this there is nothing honourable,
> hardly even any sincerity. For, *au fond*, what do you care if the
> Indian Empire is a despotism, if Indians are bullied and ex-
> ploited? You only care because the right of free speech is denied
> you. You are a creature of the despotism, a pukka sahib, tied
> tighter than a monk or a savage by an unbreakable system of
> tabus.

It is difficult to believe of the Flory we are actually shown that
his anti-imperialist feelings are merely selfish; but the point,
once more, is to qualify the possibilities of explicit commitment by insisting upon the 'unbreakable' bond between moral
judge and the situation judged, by seeing man as a puppet of
his environment. The pattern of involvement and repulsion
becomes a vicious circle: Flory is repelled by his own compromised involvement, and this is as much the source of his anger
as any 'objective' criticism of the colonialist system; yet the
anger is in that sense egoistic—'You care only because the right
of free speech is denied you'—and so is not to be trusted, lapsing
back into a sullen acceptance of the *status quo*. Flory, one feels,

is right to distrust his anger: the blurred, abstractly violent image of 'drowning their Empire in blood' revealingly indicates its subjective quality. Yet the implication is then that considered moral judgements, which transcend an immediate condition and the raw response it evokes, are impossible. As in later Orwell novels, it is a choice between some vague, vicariously fulfilling image of apocalyptic destruction (the suppressed yearning for the bombs in *Coming Up For Air*), and the wry sense of 'realistic' impotence which continually undermines it. Escape from being a creature of one's environment is possible through Romantic gestures or courageous moral commitments, and these cannot be wholly repudiated because they link one, in the midst of corruption, to one's 'better self'. Yet they are not only bound to fail, but also detach one from 'normal' life into damaging moral isolation: 'it is a corrupting thing to live one's real life in secret. One should live with the stream of life, not against it.' To strike a radical stance in a conservative society is to risk the loss of identity, since identity is still located among the old, established customs and decencies, and Orwell could not trust to an idea of identity discovered through a *collective* rejection. And so Flory tells Dr Veraswami that 'You've got to be a pukka sahib or die, in this country'. He criticises the system—'if we are a civilising influence, it's only to grab on a larger scale'—but from the vantage-point of an emotional and unarguable attachment to the old, primitive Burma which qualifies the value of his criticisms.

It is perhaps worth pointing out, at this stage, that there is a striking parallel between *Burmese Days* and Graham Greene's *The Heart of the Matter*, which is discussed in the following chapter. The resemblance lies not only in remarkable congruencies of setting and narrative detail—the seedy colonialist context, the machinations of a corrupt native leader, the arrival of a young English girl, the culminating suicide—but in the instructive parallels between Flory and Henry Scobie. Both Flory and Scobie are morally superior to their environments, yet both are corrupted by a guilty sense of collusion which narrows their awareness of what virtue they have, and so inhibits decisive moral action:

> 'Cur, spineless cur,' Flory was thinking to himself; without heat, however, for he was too accustomed to the thought. 'Sneaking, idling, boozing, fornicating, soul-examining, self-pitying cur. All those fools at the Club, those dull louts to whom you are so pleased to think yourself superior—they are all better than you, every man of them. At least they are men in their oafish way. Not cowards, not liars. Not half-dead and rotting. But you—'

This self-castigation occurs after Flory has lacked courage to defend his Burmese friend before his compatriots; and it arises because the ethic of 'honesty' turns against Flory himself. The racialists at the English club are at least 'sincere', whereas Flory himself lives a deception. They may be 'oafish', but they have at least a sort of blunt, masculine integrity which Flory, with his ceaseless 'soul-examining', does not; they are 'dull louts', but their dullness renders them safely impervious to the 'Nancy' poet style of self-pitying introspection. It is here that Flory differs decisively from Greene's Scobie. Scobie's self-castigation is intended to convince us, negatively, of his unusual humility and so of his goodness; Flory, who is much more directly a projection of the younger Orwell himself, manifests his author's own guilty self-hatred and uncertainty. The men at the club are dull, but they are also (in a significant Orwellian epithet) 'decent'; they may be bigoted and violent but, the novel insists, they are not corrupted, wallowingly self-indulgent, tremulously sensitive, like Flory himself. And part of Orwell wants to affirm this judgement, to approve Flory's self-disgust: a 'tough', masculine honesty is once more stressed as superior to objective moral discriminations, to the point where a racialist is excused on the grounds of his sincerity. The choice is between a dull, seedy world of 'decent' normality, which can be sworn at, mocked and caricatured but not wholly disapproved of, and a sensitive, isolated self-examination which rides dangerously near to the hated 'Nancy' poets, picking over their own fine emotions. As with Wells's Mr Polly, too much introspection is dangerous: it allows chaos to infiltrate and undermine the ordinary universe.

Burmese Days is hesitant in its choice of these alternatives, and its total attitude is correspondingly uncertain. There is, for instance, the problem of deciding precisely how much validity to allow to Flory's introspections: the problem of steering a safe course between unmanly sensitivity on the one hand and the straight philistinism of Elizabeth Lackersteen or Verrall, the arrogant army officer, on the other. The fluctuations of tone emerge in the following passage:

> Flory leaned over the gate. . . . Some lines from Gilbert came into his mind, a vulgar silly jingle but appropriate—something about 'discoursing on your complicated state of mind'. Gilbert was a gifted little skunk. Did all his trouble, then, simply boil down to that? Just complicated, unmanly whinings; poor-little-rich-girl stuff? . . . And if so, did that make it any more bearable? It is not the less bitter because it is perhaps one's own fault, to see oneself drifting, rotting, in dishonour and horrible futility, and all the while knowing that somewhere within one there is the possibility of a decent human being.
>
> Oh well, God save us from self-pity! Flory went back to the veranda. . . .

The jingle is 'vulgar' and Gilbert is a 'skunk'; but with these essential, distancing reservations safely made, the voice of English middle-class banality can be seriously attended to as appropriate. Once the significant status of Flory's experience has thus been denied, it is as quickly re-established in the following sentences, until the final gesture intervenes curtly to re-consolidate 'common sense'. The problem is really intractable: either Flory is to be taken seriously or he is not, and each possibility conflicts with an aspect of Orwell's intentions.

There are other ambiguities in the novel. It is difficult, for instance, to square Flory's sense of the manly integrity of his fellow-colonialists with his previous remarks to Dr Veraswami about their self-deceptive pretentiousness; and it is generally difficult to accommodate Flory's forgiving estimations of them, in the light of his own guilt, to what we are shown of their actual brutality. One is forced to conclude that, when Orwell is actually presenting the men at the English club, he indulges his criticism to the full; but when the spotlight moves to Flory and his compatriots recede into the background, they gain a vicarious merit. The continuing conflict within Orwell's own mind, between an impulse to lonely and defiant moral gesture and a sense of the collective decency of drably normative life, goes unresolved. The first can find a vent for real criticism only at the cost of suggesting a corrupting self-indulgence and callow 'ideologising'; the second is admired for its ordinariness, its shrewdly realist refusal of large gestures, but cursed and hated for its petty sterility. In almost all of Orwell's novels, this dialectic hardens into deadlock: 'ordinary' living is mocked and caricatured through the dehumanising eye of a more intelligent observer, who is himself deflated—reduced to normality—by his own or others' scepticism.

When Flory first appears in the novel, our attention is drawn to the disfiguring birthmark which stains his left cheek. The birthmark isolates him socially from others, marking him out as an exile and even a freak; but it is also at the root of that sensitivity which emerges, especially in his doomed relationship with Elizabeth Lackersteen, as his most admirable quality. The birthmark is connected both with his sensitivity and with his habit of passive compromise:

> Meanwhile, Flory had signed a public insult to his friend. He had done it for the same reason as he had done a thousand such things in his life; because he lacked the small spark of courage that was needed to refuse. For, of course, he could have refused if he had chosen; and equally, of course, refusal would have meant a row! The nagging, the jeers! At the very thought of it he flinched; he could feel his birthmark palpable on his cheek, and something happened in his throat that made his voice go flat and guilty.

Flory, who has carried his disfigurement through years of schoolboy taunts, is a victim, not just of Anglo-Burma, but of life; and the upshot of this is to contribute to the ambivalence with which he is characterised. On the one hand, this agonised awareness of his ugliness half-excuses his compromise: the responsibility for his failure to act by moral principle began, not with him, but 'in his mother's womb'. So in this respect, the birthmark is a telling detail which the novel can mobilise in support of its thesis that moral stances are impracticable. By selecting a hero stamped from birth with the insignia of failure and hypersensitivity, it suggests that Flory's weakness is in the 'nature of things' rather than in his response to a particular moral situation. But the birthmark also makes Flory non-typical, estranged at the outset from 'normal' human life: Elizabeth comes finally to hate him 'as she would have hated a leper or a lunatic'. So the scar dignifies Flory, lending him a compassion superior to others, but only at the cost of implying that he—and men like him—are really 'half-men'—freaks. And this, again, is detrimental to the validity of his criticisms of others. It is a choice between the 'normal', insensitive man— Verrall and his kind—and the lonely eccentric. There is no suggestion that a 'normal' man could take up the critical position which Flory assumes: his criticism is a function of his isolation, his desperate need to be understood, which is in turn a function of his bachelorhood, and that of his disfigurement. The novel certainly goes a good way towards endorsing Flory's raging at imperialism; but it suggests, simultaneously, that the anger is privately motivated, the gesture of a man who is out of the ordinary, and to that extent not a reliably 'objective' critic of the system. It is finally the birthmark, and not differences of ideology, which seems to Elizabeth her main reason for rejecting Flory: 'It was, finally, the birthmark that had damned him'. The two elements (the birthmark and ideological conflict) are, of course, closely interrelated in Flory's history; but the fact that the genetic issue finally predominates over the social question seems to throw the burden of Flory's tragedy, not on to his moral and political conflicts with his fellow-countrymen, but on to what he physically and unchangeably is.

In this and in other ways, *Burmese Days* is really less a

considered critique of imperialism than an exploration of private guilt, incommunicable loneliness and loss of identity for which Burma becomes at points little more than a setting. The pain which Flory suffers is 'the pain of exile'; but because that exile, by virtue of the birthmark, goes 'deeper' than social causes, criticism of the imperialist system is again tempered by a sense of overriding futility. Flory's view, common enough in Orwell, that political stances are merely temperamental rationalisations, is more or less endorsed, to the ultimate detriment of the novel's moral judgements. Despite its obvious political context, *Burmese Days*, in comparison with other of Orwell's novels, is perhaps the least directly social: what really occupies its centre is the personal relationship of Flory and Elizabeth. (It is worth adding that for this reason the novel succeeds technically more than most of the others, precisely because it avoids that direct confrontation with a social condition which in later works leads to a crude and latently unbalanced generalising. It also succeeds because Orwell, like Flory, loves Burma as much as he hates it, a fact which reveals itself in the rich precision of physical description (the landscape, the leopard-hunt), and which disappears when Orwell shifts his attention to England, which cannot, as a physical place, be loved at all.)

In the case of Flory, then, we have Orwell's earliest working of tensions and contradictions which remained painfully unresolved throughout his career as a writer. Flory can neither accept, nor disengage from, the 'normality' of a hated social system; he can refuse complicity with some of its worst aspects, but only at the cost of a compromised cynicism which reveals him as a 'half-man', a soulful and self-pitying outcast. His incapacity for decisive action works in his favour, when it is set against the arrogant certainty of a Verrall; yet this ineffectuality is also his major flaw. If he were more determinedly anti-imperialist, he would see Elizabeth Lackersteen for the callous prig she is; his inability to see this is not only exasperating in a man so sensitive to such callousness in others, but reveals the extent to which he himself shares colonialist feelings, leading him to excuse her desertion of him for Verrall. 'What right had he to be jealous? He had offered himself to a girl who was too young and pretty for him, and she had turned him down—rightly.' Elizabeth's behaviour has, in fact, little 'right' about it; but Flory can only be allowed to recognise this at the risk of self-pity. So, once more, the effort to avoid the risks of introspection leads straight into a condonement of arrogantly colonialist behaviour. There is no alternative between a full-blooded condemnation of imperialism which would involve the deceptions of self-pity and of a committed moral stance, and a rejection of self-pity, an acknowledgement of one's own complicity, which more than once blunts the edge of the criticism that part of Orwell wants to make.

If what is at stake in *Burmese Days* is an incapacity either to accept or transcend the texture of 'normal' social existence, the same can be said of Orwell's next novel, *A Clergyman's Daughter*. The novel's structure is very simple: Dorothy Hare, a rector's daughter devoted to the small duties of the parochial round, loses her memory, undergoes the experience of the Orwellian underworld (hop-picking, destitution, school-teaching), and finally returns to the rectory to continue her old life. She is rescued from the underworld life by Warburton, a middle-aged bohemian roué who wants to marry her; and the novel's crisis (in so far as it has one, given its rambling, social-documentary structure) is Dorothy's rejection of his offer. What Warburton offers her is essentially a kind of hedonist escape from the deadening trivia of the small-town parish; but although Dorothy has learnt the emptiness of this world from her London experience, and to this extent transcended its crippling limits by losing her Christian faith, an escape must be refused:

> The point is that all the beliefs I had are gone, and I've nothing to put in their place.

Warburton, the emancipated aesthete, is willing to accept and live with this lack of meaning; but Dorothy, while rejecting provincial life intellectually, is still emotionally committed to its values of work, duty, usefulness, decency: in a word, to its conformist 'normality', despite its newly revealed vacuousness. Experience and belief have proved to be incompatible; but Dorothy, while unable any longer to accept a belief which thrived simply on an ignorance of social experience, is also unable to accept a life of experience as an end in itself.

Because of this inability, the jovial generosity of Warburton comes to seem tainted, fickle, amoral: when he tries to kiss Dorothy she sees him suddenly as a 'fat, debauched bachelor'. The physical revulsion is again significant: it is really a way of simplifying the argument, in a typically Orwellian device, by linking despised moral positions to physical obscenity:

> She was in the arms of a man—a fattish, oldish man! A wave of disgust and deadly fear went through her, and her entrails seemed to shrink and freeze. His thick male body was pressing her backwards and downwards, his large, pink face, smooth, but to her eyes old, was bearing down upon her own. The harsh odour of maleness forced itself into her nostrils.

Dorothy's sexual frigidity has previously been the target of the novel's satire: it has signified her pious Anglican innocence. But now, in a sudden shift, it is used in her favour against Warburton: the virginity which the novel has emphasised as a narrowness, in its first chapters, is now enlisted in a campaign against the pressures of worldly, free-thinking emancipation. The life of the rectory is deadly and drab, but the escape which the Dickensian Christmas figure of Warburton offers must be rejected:

> When he put his arm around her it was as though he were protecting her, sheltering her, drawing her away from the brink of grey, deadly poverty and back to the world of friendly and desirable things—to security and ease, to comely houses and good clothes, to books and friends and flowers, to summer days and distant lands.

These alternatives must be denied, because the grey and deadly world, although empty and stifling, is at least *real*: it is where most people have to live, and escape is false and privileged. It is a conflict of the puritan virtues against the hedonist, and although Dorothy has undergone an experience which confirms Warburton's nihilism and casts the puritan virtues into radical question, the alternatives are Romantic and unthinkable. The full consequences of her experience cannot be faced, for there is no middle ground between narrow devotion and emancipated flippancy. Dorothy can no longer accept her world, but neither can she reject it; the movement to freedom and renewal, here as in all of Orwell's novels, ends in failure. Life is hopeless and sterile, but the worst false consciousness is to think you can change it.

Dorothy is acutely aware that what she has lost, in abandoning Christian faith, is a 'totalisation': a whole structure which can render experience intelligible, linking its smallest parochial details to a general understanding. Once this has broken under the weight of experience, no other totalisation is conceivable: 'There was, she saw clearly, no possible substitute for faith; no pagan acceptance of life as sufficient to itself, no pantheistic cheer-up stuff, no pseudo-religion of "progress" with visions of glittering Utopias and ant-heaps of steel and concrete'. She is left, simply, with the amorphous chaos of experience, which is both inferior to such totalisations in that it is meaningless, but superior in that it is 'real'. Finally, she discovers a sort of refuge in the empirical facts of experience themselves: the solution to her difficulty emerges as the stock Victorian response of 'get(ting) on with the job that lies to hand'. And so the gently satirised attitude she had when the novel began—the brisk, spinsterish, self-sacrificial attention to minute tasks—is ultimately affirmed, as superior to a radical criticism of contemporary life which could only be, like Warburton's, that of the 'Nancy' poets: decadent, self-indulgent, eccentric and in a sense indecent. Dorothy has changed, but only in consciousness: 'It is the things that happen in your heart that matter'. And although Warburton's view of life is to that extent endorsed, his belief that it can be acted on is by the same token dismissed. Warburton, in fact, is a curious blend of generous wisdom and hard-boiled philandering—partly a Cheeryble, partly a Micawber or Skimpole—and both attitudes are essential: the first is a necessary criticism of Dorothy's way of life; the second heavily qualifies such criticism and so validates the escape back to the rectory. The inescapable implication is that a rejection of ordinary experience is bound to be unprincipled; yet the alternative is not that the common life is to be gladly embraced. On the contrary, the novel's way of seeing that life has from the outset connived at Warburton's distaste for human society: this, characteristically Orwellian description of one of the Rector's parishioners, for instance:

> In her ancient, bloodless face her mouth was surprisingly large, loose and wet. The underlip, pendulous with age, slobbered forward, exposing a strip of gum and a row of false teeth as yellow as the keys of an old piano. On the upper lip was a fringe of dark, dewy moustache. . . .

Ordinary experience is physically disgusting, but the disgust must be painfully overcome, as Dorothy conquers her repugnance at rubbing embrocation into an old lady's legs. It is just that any articulate formulation of this repugnance, such as Warburton makes, must be inhibited by the pressure of guilt: the feeling that the 'grey, dead' life, however obscene, is where one really belongs.

Dorothy, then, escapes from the limiting perspectives of the rectory into an underground world of broader experience; yet what she gains from that broadening is ambiguous. On the one hand, it must be enough to expose the unreal pieties of the rectory, to allow access to the true emptiness of reality; yet on the other hand it must not be permitted to subvert too deeply a commitment to that life to which she can return. Part of the novel's technique for sustaining this balance is to be found in the process by which Dorothy enters and inhabits the world of hop-picking and vagrancy. Somehow, the novel has to introduce her into this sphere other than by her own conscious decision: for such a decision would not only be mysteriously obscure in the light of her previous, respectably devotional existence, but would also signify the sort of definitive critical rejection of that existence from which extrication back into the rectory would prove difficult. So the novel selects the simple, improbable device of translating Dorothy from the Suffolk rectory to the back-streets of London by a sudden loss of memory, silently eliding the physical process which this dramatic transition involves. Once Dorothy is immersed in this confused amnesiac state, two concomitant problems can be overcome. First, because she moves in a 'dazed, witless' trance, a 'contented and unreflecting state', the question of adequate motivation for her unlikely behaviour in travelling with petty criminals to Kent can be suspended; she can, as it were, undergo the whole 'underground' experience of the younger Orwell himself without our questioning the probability of this in terms of her pious and spinsterly temperament. More importantly, by avoiding the *conscious* critical choice which directed Orwell's own callowly Romantic 'low-life' explorations, Dorothy is not required to question her previous history in a way which would cause difficulties over her final return to it. The loss-of-memory gambit simply effects a neat transition from rectory to common lodging-house without raising the complicated issues of motive and purpose which, as a *conscious* process, this would inevitably involve.

Secondly, because of the amnesia, the whole episode takes on the quality of a dream. In this state, 'You act and plan and suffer, and yet all the while it is as though everything were a little out of focus, a little unreal'. Dorothy is a sort of automaton, moving with uncritical and unreflective contentment in a world of grotesquely unfamiliar experience. The consequence of this is to diminish the solid significance of what experience she has, in a way which allows her final return to the rectory to appear as a re-assumption of 'normal' life after an interim and unaccountable suspension of it. There is, in other words, a genuine though submerged question in the novel about the status of her underworld adventures: is this the 'reality' which the small

Suffolk town deceptively concealed, or is it an unreal interpolation, a salutary but eccentric fantasy? It is the question we
put to the novelist who stands behind much of Orwell's work
and who is detectable in some of the characterisations of this
book: is Fagin, or Brownlow, 'real' life?

There is a sense in which the novel wants to assert both attitudes at once. It is essential that the underworld should be sufficiently 'real' to disclose the lying pretensions of bourgeois
normality; yet the alternatives to that normality, whether
'above' it, in the cosmopolitanism of Warburton, or 'below'
it, in the world of tramps and prostitutes, must at the same time
be exposed as in some sense 'unreal': as unreliably untypical
diversions from the ordinary universe. And so Warburton is
presented as two-dimensional, and the criminal underworld
assumes a quality of fantasy, through the befuddled mind of
Dorothy. Because of that befuddlement, she is able to 'experience' the broader world, but without reflecting critically upon
it; it is noticeable that we are nowhere shown her actual
responses to her adventures, but allowed to see her only from
the outside. And so the final conclusions she draws are restricted:
she has learnt from the underworld the unreality of ordinary
life, but only because she has also seen the emptiness of the
wider life, which is thus not in any sense an alternative. Like
Flory, she is caught between an overwhelming sense of the
falsity of contemporary society and a consciousness of the
dangers involved in formulating that sense into anything
which might resemble a 'position'.

III

Orwell's pre-war development, from *Burmese Days* and *A
Clergyman's Daughter* to *Keep the Aspidistra Flying* and *Coming
Up For Air*, reflects his movement towards an increasingly
explicit, more frontal engagement with the tensions which
preoccupied him; but it registers, for related reasons, an ac-

celerating artistic decline. As the central dilemmas become less oblique and more urgently intractable, the treatment becomes significantly cruder, the impulse to violent, cursing caricature and uncontrolled loathing progressively less resistible. As the pressures of a disintegrating society, moving quickly to the brink of war, are increasingly taken, the qualities which distinguished *Burmese Days* and even parts of the notably inferior *A Clergyman's Daughter*—the acute sense of physically active life, the shrewd feeling for social detail—become overwhelmed by a generalising rhetoric. The sense of social reality is still alive in the childhood scenes of *Coming Up For Air*; but it has taken the form of rambling, unstructured social-documentary observation which cannot be significantly related in feeling or quality to contemporary life.

One index of this growing loss of control is the changed relation between author and protagonist: the degree of objectivity possible in the presentation of Flory or Dorothy dwindles damagingly in the later instances of Gordon Comstock and George Bowling. This is not, of course, to suggest that Comstock, in *Keep the Aspidistra Flying*, is uncritically characterised: rather that what is criticised in him is essentially what Orwell criticises in himself, and that in this respect he does not cease to be a too-direct projection of his author's own confused and unachieved attitudes. Gordon's dogmatic rejection of capitalism for an underworld existence is seen as impossibly histrionic— 'The poet starving in a garret—but starving, somehow, not uncomfortably—that was his vision of himself'—yet his modes of feeling are nevertheless strongly endorsed. Comstock's dehumanising perception is essentially Orwell's: 'The pink doll-faces of upper-class women gazed at him through the car window. Bloody nit-witted lapdogs. Pampered bitches dozing on their chains. Better the lone wolf than the cringing dog.' In this way, the novel's criticism of its hero is a regulative factor: it allows Orwell to indulge his own less intelligent feelings under the cover of critical detachment from them. The self-pity which was generally avoided in the case of Flory is now either directly unleashed ('It was the feeling of helplessness . . . of being set aside, ignored—a creature not worth worrying about'), or sidestepped only in a way which is really just a more subtle form of the same emotion, coated with a desperate 'realism': 'He was thirty, moth-eaten, and without charm. Why should any girl ever look at him again?'

By virtue of Gordon's belief that money is the all-determining factor in every human feeling and relationship, the novel is able to maintain the tension between a criticism of the formal, ordinary world and a criticism of attempts to escape it. If the ordinary world is corrupted by money, then a committed stance against it will also be financially undermined. So commitment will fail absurdly, but not in a way which reflects any particular credit on the established society. Moreover, once Gordon's money-doctrine is accepted, we are persuaded to half-excuse his more self-indulgent behaviour—his callous treatment of his girl-friend Rosemary, for example—because lack of money becomes a covering formula for all types of weakness: 'Social failure, artistic failure, sexual failure—they are all the same. And lack of money is at the bottom of them all.' In believing this, Gordon is holding an attitude which merely reflects the views of the bourgeois world: he is, in this respect, thoroughly endorsing bourgeois values, bound to the world he rejects by a simple inversion. Gordon rejects middle-class society from what are essentially middle-class premises: his extraordinary sensitivity to such matters as the social significance of kinds of doorbell indicates the depth of his obsession with the insignia of a social structure he is supposed to reject. The important point is that Gordon, in subscribing to a financial estimation of human qualities ('No woman ever judges a man by anything except his income'), dehumanises men as thoroughly as does the society he assaults. He would dismiss the view that, even within the corruptions of capitalism, men are still men, and their relationships can still partially transcend the crude determinants which limit them, as 'unrealistic' humanitarianism; and the novel, at least at points, would seem to confirm his attitude. Like Orwell himself, Gordon oscillates between Romantic gesture and a cynical accommodation to the *status quo*, seeing no other possible standpoint; like Orwell, he is anti-Romantic in the way that only a confirmed Romantic can be.

It is significant, in the light of the choices offered in the novel, that Gordon's ideological opponent is not an experienced working-class socialist, but Ravelston, the rich, guilty, middle-class left-winger. The result is a typically Orwellian conflict between the amorphous complexities of sordid 'experience' on the one hand and the abstract rigidities of 'ideology' on the other. 'Ravelston . . . knew . . . that life under a decaying capitalism is deathly and meaningless. But this knowledge was only theoretical. You can't really *feel* that kind of thing when your income is eight hundred a year.' Gordon's 'front-line' defence against socialism, then, is an appeal to the immovable misery of his own life; but his 'second line' defence is a cynical acknowledgement, in the manner of Flory, that his arguments are in any case only the arbitrary projections of private feeling. He attacks Ravelston's socialist argument, but then, in a second move, detaches himself cynically from his own scepticism:

> 'All this about Socialism and Capitalism and the state of the modern world and God knows what. I don't give a —— for the state of the modern world. If the whole of England was starving except myself and the people I care about, I wouldn't give a damn.'
> 'Don't you exaggerate just a little?'
> 'No. All this talk we make—we're only objectifying our own feelings. It's all dictated by what we've got in our pockets. . . .'

Gordon is forced to deny the validity of his own experience, since even this leads him towards a (purely negative) 'position'; in order to express the full quality of his cynicism he must at the same time negate it by suggesting that it is, after all, purely subjective and so valueless. He is, of course, correct—his pessimism *is* a subjective projection—yet at the same time the novel's own way of looking works to suggest an at least partial endorsement of the view that 'It's all dictated by what we've got in our pockets'. The novel is thus vulnerable to a serious criticism: in order to affirm the validity of Gordon's dramatic rejection of society, it must show his evaluation to be objectively true; but in order to protect both itself and its hero from the dangers of declared moral commitment, it must at the same time deny the objective validity of the position it takes. The uncertainty registers itself, once more, in a fluctuation of attitude within the text:

> He gazed out at the graceless streets. At this moment it seemed to him that in a street like this, in a town like this, every life that is lived must be meaningless and intolerable. The sense of disintegration, of decay, that is endemic in our time, was strong upon him. Somehow it was mixed up with the ad-posters opposite. . . . Corner Table grins at you, seemingly optimistic, with a flash of false teeth. But what is behind the grin? Desolation, emptiness, prophecies of doom. . . . The great death-wish of the modern world. Suicide pacts. Heads stuck in gas-ovens in lonely maisonettes. French letters and Amen pills. . . . It is all written in Corner Table's face.

The vision of meaninglessness begins as Gordon's own: this is how it 'seemed to him', and the novel does not rush instantly to confirm his view. His attitude belongs to the decay of the times, which lends it more solid substantiation but still leaves it open to question. Then, as the passage gathers speed, it is no longer clear whether the speaking voice is Comstock's or Orwell's: what began as a character's attitude is generalised to an image of society which seems, in the dogmatism of the final sentence, to have been finally established as 'objective'.

Similar ambiguities can be found throughout the book. Gordon's stance is revealed as deliberately self-indulgent—'He clung with a sort of painful joy to the notion that because he was poor everyone must *want* to insult him'—yet, equally, the significance of his experience seems confirmed: 'He perceived that it is quite impossible to explain to any rich person, even to anyone so decent as Ravelston, the essential bloodiness of poverty'. There can, in other words, be no traffic between the raw stuff of experience and the categories of understanding and analysis; like Flory, Gordon insists on the inherent incommunicability of his deprivation, the impossibility of ever being understood, as a way of avoiding an articulate formulation of his experience which might involve him in a 'commitment'— to changing the society, for instance. The experience remains jealously private, a mode of defiant self-definition against the world. This attitude is certainly criticised; but because Gordon's poverty is real, a critic of his behaviour is placed, for lack of an alternative standpoint, in the shoes of Ravelston. He can risk criticism of Gordon's attitudes only at the cost of a damaging charge of patrician remoteness from the realities of Gordon's existence.

The choice which the novel poses, then, is essentially that defined by Flory in *Burmese Days*: one must either be a pukka sahib or die. 'Serve the money-god or go under: there is no other rule.' It is a sharper choice than that in *A Clergyman's Daughter*, where the belief still lingered that an external accommodation to society could be made in a way which preserved an interior consciousness from its falsehoods. In *Aspidistra* this posture is much less viable: if attitudes are so mechanically determined by economic environment (and Gordon's belief is that kind of vulgarisation of Marxism), then there can be no balanced compromise. Gordon must finally re-enter society, impelled, significantly, by the forces of 'decency'. That decency is embodied both in Ravelston (who throughout the novel symbolises one side of Orwell as Gordon symbolises another: the generous, wryly 'realist' compromiser as against the self-indulgent Romantic), and also in Rosemary, who is to bear Gordon's child. The money-god cannot be fought 'when he gets at you through your sense of decency'; the struggle between the impulse to determined moral commitment and the undermining claims of a weary 'common sense' is decided in favour of the latter.

Yet it is not decided without considerable ambiguity.

Gordon's return to society suggests the impracticality of his venture into a social limbo without, however, too radically questioning the validity of that venture. It also indicates the inevitability of a return to routine social life without implying either that this is a sort of betrayal or that it is deeply valuable. Gordon's plan has been to sink low enough in the social structure to free himself from bourgeois claims: 'Down in the safe soft womb of earth, where there is no getting of jobs or losing of jobs, no relatives or friends to plague you, no hope, fear, ambition, honour, duty. . . . That was where he wished to be.' It is a way of negating the whole range of common drives and feelings without particularly having to act: a passive subsiding into social death, into the fertile darkness at the base of society. This, as Ravelston points out, is a 'mistake': one can't live in a corrupt society and escape corruption. Yet it is not particularly suggested that this mode of 'social' protest is inherently inadequate: a capitulation rather than a constructive challenge; a selfishly individualist rather than a collective transcendence; a false idealising of those at the end of the social scale who seem to Gordon most free from oppression but who are in reality most deeply exploited. It is merely suggested that such a gesture might be possible for saints, but not for Gordon.

On the one hand, the return to lower middle-class life is seen as a compromise (Gordon will 'sell his soul' to his firm); but it is also seen, suddenly, as a return to 'decent, fully human life', in a way which is difficult to square with the descriptions of that life elsewhere in the novel:

> He wondered about the people in houses like this. They would be, for example, small clerks, shop-assistants, commercial travellers, insurance touts, tram conductors. Did *they* know that they were only puppets dancing when money pulled the strings? You bet they didn't. And if they did, what would they care? They were too busy being born, being married, begetting, working, dying. It mightn't be a bad thing, if you could manage it, to feel yourself one of them, one of the ruck of men. Our civilisation is founded on greed and fear, but in the lives of

common men the greed and fear are mysteriously transmuted into something nobler. The lower middle-class people in there, behind their lace curtains, with their children and their scraps of furniture and their aspidistras—they lived by the money-code, sure enough, and yet they contrived to keep their decency. The money-code as they interpreted it was not merely cynical and hoggish. They had their standards, their inviolable points of honour. They 'kept themselves respectable'—kept the aspidistra flying. Besides, they were *alive*. They were bound up in the bundle of life. They begot children, which is what the saints and the soul-savers never by any chance do.

The transitions of attitude here are interesting. 'Ordinary' life is still seen externally, as a kind of curiosity, and the physical setting of the meditation (Gordon is looking at a street of houses) powerfully underlines the sense of a distanced analysis of the inscrutable. People are still 'puppets', and the observer thus distinguished from them by his superior insight; yet if one could plunge into the ruck of men, in a movement at once self-conscious and self-abnegating, one might perhaps find value in their lives. The lower middle class are still dehumanisingly described—notice the casual equivalence of status between lace curtains, children and furniture—but they are, at least, 'decent', and even in some nebulous sense 'alive'. We have not previously seen 'life' and 'respectability' as equivalents, but now we are asked to do so, as a way of ratifying Gordon's return. So the novel finally perceives the humanity which remains at the heart of capitalism, but chiefly, one feels, as a kind of after-thought, a tactic for rendering Gordon's surrender acceptable. Moreover, the sense of nobility in the common life is not allowed to override, even at this point, the more typically negative feelings towards it which have run throughout the novel, the patronising Orwellian contempt for the 'little' men: 'He would be a law-abiding little cit like any other law-abiding little cit—a soldier in the strap-hanging army. Probably it was better so.' Is it 'better so' because Gordon has no other choice (he feels 'as though some force outside him were pushing him'), and is thus acquitted of responsibility? Or because a denial of society, although morally admirable, is simply impractical? Or because society is, after all, of value? It is something of all of these: but the shifts of attitude obscure the issue, trying to salvage the value of social rejection while simultaneously affirming the merit of social settlement. (We do not, for instance, know how much Gordon has lost by his abandonment of poetry, and so how truly detrimental his re-integration might be, since neither we nor he can decide whether he is a good poet or a bad one.) Orwell remains ambiguously stranded between two positions: once more, an intensely emotional rejection of the decent aspidistra world clashes head-on with a sense of pragmatic decency which rejects such intense emotions as privileged luxury.

Orwell's next novel, *Coming Up For Air*, represents, not an extension, but a re-working of the problems we have examined so far. It is his most typical 'lower middle-class' novel, obsessed with the cheapness of 'suburbia', permeated by a tired, cursing, ragged defeatism and underpinned by a semi-hysterical sense of anxiety and estrangement as war approaches. The choice of the first-person narrator, George Bowling, is itself significant. Bowling is fat, seedy and disillusioned, an integral part of the decaying suburban world he criticises, yet imbued with a quality of ironic insight superior to those who surround him. There is thus, from the outset, no possibility of the experience offered by the novel being 'objectively' appraised—not only because no other character is allowed to advance an opposing viewpoint, but because Bowling's disgust with his environment is qualified by a cynically devaluing sense of his own corruption, his inert complicity in the world he despises:

> Don't mistake me. I'm not trying to put myself over as a kind of tender flower, the aching heart behind the smiling face and so forth. You couldn't get on in the insurance business if you were anything like that. I'm vulgar, I'm insensitive, and I fit in with my environment. . . . But also I've got something else inside me, chiefly a hangover from the past. . . . I'm fat, but I'm thin inside. Has it ever struck you that there's a thin man

inside every fat man, just as they say there's a statue inside every block of stone?

Bowling, an 'ordinary, middling chap', fits in with his environment: but neither so thoroughly that he cannot achieve a reflectively critical standpoint towards it, nor so loosely that he can analyse it as a whole and imagine an alternative. Through the focus of Bowling, then, the novel is able to project a criticism of society which is the more convincing because it emerges, not from the contemptible 'abstractions' of the ideologists, but from a man trapped within its limits. Yet by the same token, the criticism cannot be 'positive', since Bowling's title to criticise without arrogance or abstraction is gained from the fact that he bears around the seediness he discerns within his own grotesque physique. He is superior in insight to others, but not too much so:

> The usual crowd that you can hardly fight your way through was streaming up the pavement, all of them with that insane fixed expression on their faces that people have in London streets. . . . I felt as if I was the only person awake in a city of sleep-walkers. That's an illusion, of course. When you walk through a crowd of strangers it's next to impossible not to imagine that they're all waxworks, but probably they're thinking just the same about you.

The point of this is both to affirm and to qualify his greater perceptiveness: to allow him a partial transcendence of his environment without the deceptions of disengagement. In one sense, Bowling is presented with a greater degree of objectivity than Gordon Comstock: he is a vulgar, philandering philistine, and is seen by the novel to be so. Yet, as with Comstock, the point of this distancing is to permit Orwell to indulge his own cruder feelings—his malicious delight in cruel parody, his own sporadically philistine contempt for intellectuals, his gushingly apocalyptic despair, his desire for destructive violence—while at the same time protecting himself, by virtue of his spokesman's seedy grossness, from any direct commitment to these attitudes.

The qualities which give Bowling a right to be heard, then, are also the qualities which prevent him from achieving any meaningful organisation of his experience. The world dramatised through his eyes is fragmented and unreal: the synthetic frankfurter he swallows early in the novel symbolises an insubstantial world where everything is 'slick and streamlined, everything made out of something else'. The most interesting point at issue is not the stock quality of this judgement: whatever local force it might have looks less impressive when it is placed in the context of Bowling's pervasively jaundiced worldview, his monotonously one-dimensional perception of his environment. The significant point is that, here as in other novels, this feeling of social unreality conflicts with an opposing sense of the inert solidity of the suburban world. Bowling's perception of his society is coloured by the insistent thought of impending war: he is struck by the strangeness of the notion that the routine world of London, its houses and factories, is likely to be brought into destructive collision with an abstract world of political strategy and theory. He imagines 'bloomers soaked in blood' on a washing-line, disturbed by this connection of the domestically known and the abstractly feared. And this works both ways: to sharpen a sense of the indestructible *reality* of the experienced social world ('Miles and miles of streets, fried-fish shops, tin chapels, picture houses . . .') in contrast to the intangible forces of international politics; but also to highlight the fragile unreality of the quotidian, its vulnerability to destruction. The question, once again, is which world is more 'real'. Bowling recoils from suburbia, but satirises Porteous, his intellectual friend, for his aesthetic escapism. On the other hand, little of the same satire attaches to Bowling's own escapist and ill-fated return to Lower Binfield, his childhood home.

The ambiguity emerges most sharply in the account of the political meeting which Bowling attends in Part Three of the novel. The anti-Fascist speaker is made to seem a purveyor of mindless, ranting hatred; yet the fear of Fascism he articulates

is also Bowling's own, and Bowling can therefore equally
satirise those in the audience who cannot understand the lecture.
Both commitment and apathy are despicable: Bowling's shifts
of feeling towards the audience register the contradiction:

> So perhaps after all there *is* a significance in this mingy little
> crowd that'll turn out on a winter night to listen to a lecture of
> this kind. Or at any rate in the five or six who can grasp what
> it's all about. They're simply the outposts of an enormous army.
> They're the long-sighted ones, the first rats to spot that the ship
> is sinking. Quick, quick! The Fascists are coming! Spanners
> ready, boys! Smash others or they'll smash you. So terrified of
> the future that we're jumping straight into it like a rabbit diving
> down a boa-constrictor's throat.

The audience is 'mingy', but is grudgingly allowed a significance—a significance limited in the next breath to the few, like
Bowling himself, who can understand, and which thus pre-
serves intact a dismissive attitude towards the rest. The image
of the 'long-sighted ones' then defines that importance, but
the following image—that of the rats leaving the ship—
instantly curtails any suggestion of active virtue. Then, with
the following, hysterical phrases ('The Fascists are coming . . .'),
a fear which is in fact Bowling's most characteristic feeling is
detached from himself and projected on to the audience, as a
way of distancing himself from their, and his own, involvements. It is only the 'we' of the final sentence which acknow-
ledges (lest Bowling be given too much lonely moral distinction) that this is a common condition in which he himself is
implicated. Once more, Orwell's novel embodies a paradox:
those who escape from the ordinary world by intellectual
pursuits or political ideologies are satirised, but so also are those
who involve themselves 'mindlessly' with it. The only viable
stance is one of passive withdrawal *within* the world: the
Bowling posture, midway between fool and intellectual, law-
abiding 'cit' and radical ideologist, stupefied masses and contemptible capitalists, 'Progress' and 'Culture'. It is the classical
stance of the lower middle-class hero.

IV

In *The Road to Wigan Pier*, Orwell distinguishes between two
kinds of Socialists:

> On the one hand you have the warm-hearted unthinking
> Socialist, the typical working-class Socialist, who only wants
> to abolish poverty and does not always grasp what this implies.
> On the other hand, you have the intellectual, book-trained
> Socialist, who understands that it is necessary to throw our
> present civilisation down the sink and is quite willing to do
> so. And this type is drawn, to begin with, entirely from the
> middle class, and from a rootless town-bred section of the
> middle class at that . . . it includes . . . all that dreary tribe of
> high-minded women and sandal-wearers and bearded fruit-
> juice drinkers who come flocking towards the smell of 'progress'
> like bluebottles to a dead cat. The ordinary decent person,
> who is in sympathy with the *essential* aims of Socialism, is given
> the impression that there is no room for his kind in any
> Socialist party that means business.

Here, cast into explicitly political terms, are the horns of
Orwell's dilemma. Orwell's own socialism was essentially of
the 'warm-hearted' kind; yet because he was also a middle-
class intellectual, he understood the limits of this simple
decency, as an adequate political force. At the same time, he
was strongly enough attracted to it to detest the 'dreary tribe'
of his fellow-bourgeois socialists, without ever being able to
feel himself at home in its world. The working class is warm
and decent, but it is impossible to be 'really intimate' with
them, or even to believe that they can *think*: '. . . no genuine
working man grasps the deeper implications of Socialism'.
This, of course, was a patently false judgement, but because he
could not bring himself to disbelieve it, Orwell could see no
way to unify theory and experience. *Wigan Pier* is a sympathetic
inquiry into the lives of working people, but it is a study of
Orwell's attitudes, not of theirs: the analyses are perceptive and
sensitively detailed, but they are descriptions of environment

rather than of experience. The tone of the work veers constantly between the best qualities of Orwell's prose and a racy, generalising, Chestertonian externality which can verge, at times, on glibness.

Orwell's account of the lives of working people is external, not only because of his own, honestly declared position as a middle-class observer, but, more significantly, because they have no immediate relevance to his own dilemma. They are, from his own insecure standpoint, part of a settled, rooted, self-contained culture at the bottom of the social scale, without the desire for middle-class respectability. It is this desire which Gordon Comstock identifies, in his own relatives, as the most corrupting:

> It was not *merely* lack of money. It was rather that, having no money, they still lived mentally in the money-world—the world in which money is virtue and poverty is crime. It was not poverty but the down-dragging of *respectable* poverty that had done for them. They had accepted the money-code, and by that code they were failures. They had never had the sense to lash out and just *live*, money or no money, as the lower classes do. How right the lower classes are! Hats off to the factory lad who with fourpence in the world puts his girl in the family way! At least he's got blood and not money in his veins.

Gordon has 'never felt any pity for the poor', because 'hardship' is at least 'decent'. 'It is the black-coated poor, the middle-middle class, who need pitying.' To sink into the underworld of the industrial working class, or of tramps and prostitutes, is thus to be safe: it is, at least, a *definition*, rather than a life of deception and pretence. The inescapable suggestion of this, of course, is that the working class is secure: secure because they want nothing better than to live as they do. In his better moments, Orwell could see the sickness of this remote idealisation of the 'factory lad': he knew, as others of his class did not, that no one lives in a slum or caravan by choice. When he was thinking of the working class with this direct attention, as in parts of *Wigan Pier*, Orwell could understand this; but when he was considering the class-dilemma which touched his own situation more closely—the frustrated lower middle or impoverished upper middle class, struggling between a desired 'decency' and the real pressures of insecurity—the working class came to seem the great, impersonal, contented mass at the bottom of the social structure who were blessed because they could fall no further and had no chance of rising.

Orwell's own experience of deprivation, together with what he learnt of the ruling social class from his days in Burma, led him to a negative identification with the working class, and so to a rejection of the dominant social ideology. Yet his essentially middle-class belief in decency, of which he could find a reflection in the 'respectable' working class, detached him from any trust in the ideological formulations of socialism. 'Decency' meant the normal, the middling and the accepted; ideology meant the extreme, the eccentric, the subversive. And it seemed impossible to unite the two. If Orwell could have admitted (what is patently obvious) that it is possible for a working man to grasp the theory of socialism at a highly complex and articulate level, he would have seen the possibility of a totalisation and transcendence of the social experience he detested which was made, not abstractly, from a vantage-point of privileged externality, but from within its most immediate pressures. Because he was, in the end, too middle class to believe this, he was left with the raw material of experience on the one hand, and ideology on the other, and neither was in itself viable. The first was too caught up in the prevalent feelings of social orthodoxy, in an emotional commitment to the pieties of the present, to represent a radical alternative; the second *was* such an alternative, but only by detaching one from 'common decency', from the iron grip of the quotidian, into the hated realm of 'pansy' abstraction.

Orwell never escaped this paradox, as is clear enough from his post-war novels. But it was a paradox which went beyond his own immediate situation. It was the problem of the lower middle-class hero, too conscious of his deprivation to endorse the unreal doctrines of conservative orthodoxy or radical dissent, yet too aware of his own frustration to submit blindly to his role as creature of a hated environment. Finally, it is the problem of the lower middle-class novel as a whole: the dilemma of a class marooned between orthodox decencies and deprivation, unable either to fully accept or fully reject the social system, and so critical both of the common life and of its possible alternatives.

CHAPTER IV

Reluctant Heroes: the Novels of Graham Greene

I

AT THE end of *The Power and the Glory*, the whisky priest dismisses the half-caste who has betrayed him into the hands of the lieutenant of police with a gesture of forgiveness. 'The priest waved his hand; he bore no grudge because he expected nothing else of anything human. . . .' It is a characteristic moment in Greene, and one which demands analysis. The priest's gesture embodies a paradox: it has the quality of Christian humanity, yet that humanity is ironically dependent on an overriding sense of man's cheapness. The forgiving wave dignifies and devalues man in a single gesture: in enacting a compassionate solidarity with human corruption, it endorses, at the same time, the unchanging reality of that corruption. Yet by the same token, the sceptical disillusion which makes forgiveness automatic qualifies any suggestion of outstanding sanctity on the priest's part: it is easy to forgive creatures from whom one expects little. Greene, then, allows his whisky priest a compassionate holiness while protecting him from the dangers of pride; because the priest devalues himself, knowing the half-caste's weakness within his own body, he can be safely dignified by his author. The priest is raised above corruption without being detached from it; it is by his sense of complicity with sin that he is able partially to transcend it. Through an image of despairing forgiveness, then, Greene is able to dramatise two qualities of feeling which are everywhere deeply interrelated in his work: a pitying compassion which confirms a kind of value without thereby challenging the fact of human worthless-

ness, and a potentially heroic virtue which is at the same time
fiercely or sceptically hostile to the notion of goodness. In both
cases, it seems necessary to affirm and deny human value in the
same moment.

After his fruitless interview with Father Rank in *The Heart
of the Matter*, Scobie recognises that he is incapable of conforming to what he sees as orthodox Roman Catholicism. 'I know
the answers as well as he does. One should look after one's own
soul at whatever cost to another, and that's what I can't do,
what I shall never be able to do.' Scobie's attitude here is essentially Greene's: given a tragic tension between the claims of
human relationship and the demands of faith, the rigours of
orthodoxy must be guiltily denied in the name of the human.
The irony implicit in Greene's view, however, is more subtle
than this simple counterpoising. For although an individualist
'soul-saving' theology is rejected, the concomitant feelings
crystallised around the same phase of Roman Catholic history
—the sense of relationships as negative and treacherous, corrosive of personal integrity—are uncompromisingly retained.
Indeed they are extended, at times, into a version of the human
world as putrid corruption which moves beyond the Catholic
tradition into forms of radical Protestantism. The result is a
striking paradox: Greene's protagonists turn, at the risk of
damnation, from a soul-saving theology to the insidious pressures of humanity, but only in the context of a continually
undermining disbelief in the final validity of such claims. Orthodox Catholicism is denied in the name of 'humanism'; yet that
humanism is itself critically qualified by traditionally Catholic
ways of feeling. The upshot of this is a kind of deadlock: the
human value of men like Scobie or the whisky priest lies in
their readiness to reject an orthodoxy in which they nevertheless continue to believe; yet to acknowledge the superior truth
of that orthodoxy, in the act of refusing it, is to confront the
inadequacy of the sheerly human commitments they embrace.

By affirming an absolute standard, then, Greene's characters
are able to retain a sceptical detachment from human values:

a detachment which lends them superiority, in the final analysis, to the rationalist or liberal humanist. Yet by failing that standard in action while endorsing it in consciousness, they can reveal qualities of compassion which are again superior to the humanist's ethic by virtue of the disillusion and damnation— and so lack of self-deception—in which they are rooted. To go through the motions of human love, in a nagging awareness of its inevitable partiality, emerges as a more courageously mature and disinterested attitude than that of the humanist, who trusts naïvely and destructively to an ultimate value in man. By a curious irony, scepticism, *dégagement* and disbelief furnish a more positive ethic than a committed faith in the possibilities of human good. The fundamental detachment from the mess of secular complexities which permits the Christian a deeper insight than the humanist also allows him to outstrip the humanist on his own territory.

The point may be usefully illustrated by *The Heart of the Matter*. Here, as in all Greene's novels, human relationship is inherently tragic: love, pity and innocence are lethal because they entice men out of their safely sterile *dégagements* into the corrupting complicities of passion and responsibility, into infectious and conflicting involvements which proliferate beyond control. This is the thesis which the novel is intended to illustrate, and it centres on Scobie because he alone is agonisedly conscious of the inescapable debt and damage implicit in the vulnerabilities of feeling. Because the thesis is given rather than argued, we are asked to admire Scobie's moral pragmatism: his sluggish, compassionate enactment of the motions of relationship, constantly penetrated by a desire for the peace of death, is offered as wiser than that ethic of decisive action which can belong only to the innocent, to those damagingly ignorant of the heart of the matter. Yet what is obvious in the novel is that this tragic version of life is the result, as well as the motivation, of Scobie's behaviour: his well-intentioned bungling, his rejection of truth for a patching-up of immediate pain which merely delays and complicates decision, his despairing half-

commitment and wry passivity, his self-disgusted inability to
value himself, his complicity in allowing others to live a lie,
his sentimental attraction to suffering, his disbelief in the possibility of happiness—all these are offered as *responses* to a given
hopelessness, but are, just as much, the sources of that paralysis.
Scobie acts as he does because he sees the human condition as
irreparable, but it is at least partially true that the human condition of the novel is irreparable because he acts as he does. (It
is perhaps worth mentioning that the aspect of traditional
Christian ethics which Scobie finds most unpalatable—their
apparently intransigent insistence on the need to take a stand
in certain situations at the cost of immediate damage—is related
to a belief that the alternative is likely to be the kind of mess in
which Scobie finds himself.) Because human relationships are
viewed as inherently unviable, moral blame attaches, not
chiefly to Scobie himself, but to the 'conditions of life'; relationships fail 'naturally', evil spreads by its own momentum, and
what is then in question is not the quality of action, but the
nature of intention, despite its inevitably negative effects. In
this continuing concern with motive rather than effect, Greene
is, ironically, very Roman Catholic in attitude. It is necessary
that Scobie's efforts to redeem his situation should fail, since
this validates the novel's thesis; but it is also essential that he
should fail with good intentions, since this allows him a moral
superiority to his situation without suggesting the possibility of
a transforming morality which might effectively challenge that
condition. Scobie's 'anti-heroism', his failure to conform to his
own absolute standard, is the source of his humanism, and thus
of a moral worth greater than others—than his trivially
malicious fellow-colonialists, for instance. Yet his conscious
commitment to the standard he betrays both critically qualifies
the humanism, lending him a perspective beyond its limits, and
intensifies the price he pays for humane action in a way which
renders it even more admirable. Once more, an affirmation of
human goodness is accompanied with strict reservations about
its validity.

Greene's 'bad' Catholics, then, condemn themselves by the rigour of an absolute orthodoxy while consciously breaking its rules. Sanctity, like the damnation of Pinkie in *Brighton Rock*, consists in recognising and refusing the rules simultaneously; the two conditions are allied in this as in other respects. The characters' failure to conform to the standard is essential for humane action; their continued acceptance of it is necessary, not only if they are to be distinguished from non-Christian humanists, but if they are to experience that self-deprecating humility of failure which is, for Greene, the condition of holiness. The standard is refused in the name of the corrupting complexities of routine experience; yet precisely because that experience is still seen, from the standpoint of orthodoxy, as tangled, amorphous and self-defeating, it provides no basis for the formulation of any alternative ethic by which a man could press through to a questioning of orthodoxy itself. Orthodoxy is submitted to the test of experience, and its inadequacies exposed: but not to the point where it might be shown up as hollow—revealed, for instance, as bad theology—for that would be to slacken the tension between orthodoxy and humanity, and so to destroy that guilty self-disgust by which the believer is rendered superior to the rationalist. The orthodox standard reveals itself in a mainly negative way: in the characters' guilty scrupulousness in offending against it. Their anxiety at being bad Catholics is one of their most notably Catholic traits.

The novels, then, have to preserve a very fine tension between their characters' conscious commitment to orthodoxy and their active rejection of its limits. Yet there is more than one occasion where the effort to sustain the tension leads them into serious ambiguity and confusion. The behaviour of the priest in *The Power and the Glory* is a case in point. If the priest is to be saintly, he must infringe the orthodoxy; yet if he is to have the self-castigating humility of holiness, he must also remain convinced of its truth. The novel does not everywhere succeed in persuading us of the logicality of this paradox. In the prison scene, for instance, when the priest is confronted with the intolerably pious complacency of the middle-aged woman beside him in the darkness, he is almost able to articulate his 'unorthodoxy' into an affirmative argument which could undermine the falsity of the woman's religious respectability. He refuses, for example, to accept her dogmatic assertion that the sexual intercourse of the couple in the dark corner of the cell is mortal sin, and allows only that 'We don't know. It may be.' Yet although he is here on the point of formulating his superior depth of experience into a 'position', his criticism of established religion must not be allowed to develop into a radical assault, for this would be to deprive him of the very standard by which he measures his own humble unworthiness, and so the means by which he achieves a kind of heroism. Yet the problem persists: if the priest is able to extend forgiving leniency to the sexual sins of others, why is he unable to do this in his own case? The priest is extraordinarily stringent with himself, but ceaselessly liberal with others; he can perceive the bad faith of respectable Catholicism and its pressing dangers to the soul, but is at the same time gripped with scruples for such things as saying mass in mud-huts without an altar stone. The ambiguity is also evident at another point: in his self-accusation of sins which we are forced to take on credence because they are nowhere shown in the novel. 'The words proud, lustful, envious, cowardly, ungrate-ful . . . he was all these things.' There is a genuine obscurity here: either the priest is accurate in his self-evaluation, in which case his apparent virtue is cast damagingly into question; or he is self-deceived, in which case the novel can impress us with his humility only at the cost of implying in him a disturbing and ultimately unaccountable lack of insight. The novel effectively refuses to choose: either possibility would harm the image of the whisky priest which it is concerned to project. One is forced to conclude that the priest's self-estimation cannot really be true, since it obstinately refuses to accommodate itself to the novel's actual presentation of him; but neither can it really be false, since the authenticity of the priest's experience depends upon our giving at least some credence to the accuracy of his judgements and the reality of his sense of failure. To deny this is to conclude that the priest's perceptive insight into the condition of others consorts mysteriously with a peculiar obtuseness in his view of himself—an obtuseness which the term 'humility' is too indiscriminate to cover.

Yet 'humility' is, of course, the formal explanation which the novel offers for this incongruency: the priest's overbearing sense of inadequacy as a man of God. That inadequacy, however, lies largely in infringements of an orthodoxy which he recognises as actively harmful in the case of the woman prisoner, or, later in the novel, in the bourgeois religion of the hygienically Lutheran Lehrs. It is his humility which prevents him from pressing through his sense of these falsities into anything which might approach a radical criticism: he believes that the woman prisoner needs sympathy, not correction. Yet in emphasising this humility as his virtue, the novel also covertly indulges in the priest what is really a kind of defectiveness, akin to his nervous giggling and card-tricks; it exploits the priest's inability to take himself seriously in order to ward off criticisms of the Church, while at the same time giving the priest's experience a serious value. The novel, in other words, needs to endorse the significance of its protagonist's experience, but needs to prevent him from doing the same. The humility is part of a general experience which objectively aims a radical criticism at orthodoxy, but it is simultaneously used to forestall any subjective appropriation of such criticism on the part of the priest himself—a move which might lead the novel and its hero into the camp of the revolutionary lieutenant of police. When the priest confronts the lieutenant before his death, the novel's attitude is less than candid: the priest agrees, briefly and unspecifically, with the lieutenant's attack on the established Church, but then affirms the superiority of the Christian faith:

> 'What an excuse it all was, what a fake. Sell all and give to the poor—that was the lesson, wasn't it? And Senora so-and-so, the druggist's wife, would say the family wasn't really deserv-

ing of charity, and Senor This, That and the Other would say that if they starved, what else did they deserve, they were Socialist anyway, and the priest—you—would notice who had done his Easter duty and paid his Easter offering. . . .'

The priest said, 'You are so right'. He added quickly, 'Wrong too, of course. . . .'

'Well, we have ideas too,' the lieutenant was saying. No more money for saying prayers, no more money for building places to say prayers in. We'll give people food instead, teach them to read, give them books. We'll see they don't suffer.'

'But if they want to suffer. . . . We have facts, too, we don't try to alter—that the world's unhappy whether you are rich or poor—unless you are a saint and there aren't many of those. It's not worth bothering too much about a little pain here. . . .'

The area of real agreement between priest and policeman—their common dislike of established religion—is quickly blurred over, and the differences sharpened. The priest's callous attitude to suffering can be made more palatable by an appeal to his experience—he, after all, has known pain, and so his last statement can be made to seem courageous rather than cruel—but it is really a kind of trick. We are persuaded, by the depth and value of the priest's experience, to accept from his mouth an attitude we would be less willing to take from the pious clerics whose way of life he has renounced; and yet the statement is the kind of platitude which belongs essentially to their world. The novel appeals to the priest's wisdom only as a way of asking us to accept the persuasions of an orthodoxy which it has been part of that wisdom to criticise. So, once more, humane values are both affirmed and heavily qualified: the whisky priest is revealed as superior to bourgeois pieties by virtue of his humane compassion, but superior to humanism by virtue of his identification with orthodox piety. A precariously narrow line must be balanced between a rejection of love, and a belief that it can be in any sense effective.

There are similar unresolved ambiguities in almost all of Greene's 'Catholic' novels. Why in any case does the unheroic whisky priest stay in the country at the risk of his life? Why does Scobie stay in his African colony? Why does Sarah Miles, in *The End of the Affair*, make a vow to a God she doesn't believe in? Why does she see herself as 'a bitch and a fake'? Why does Querry, in *A Burnt-Out Case*, stay overnight in the forest to comfort his injured servant Deo Gratias? At the root of all these questions lies a common problem. Each of these facts counts to the credit of the character concerned: in different ways, they are evidence of moral distinction, of a capacity for some kind of love. Yet love, in the world of Greene's novels, is an even more treacherous passion than pity: 'I don't believe in anyone who says love, love, love,' says Louise Scobie, in response to the self-dramatising advances of Wilson: 'It means self, self, self.' And this is an attitude which Greene's novels on the whole endorse. Love is a self-regarding emotion or a destructive possessiveness; it is innocent of the reality of failure, and so dangerously naïve, finally indistinguishable from egoism. There is no alternative in Greene's world between the diseased compassion of a Scobie, dissolving the self's integrity into the shapelessness of a growing stain, and the callow self-assertiveness of a Wilson or the public-school bumptiousness of a Bagster. Each of the novels, then, confronts a crucial difficulty. If God's love is real, it must be in some sense incarnated in human living: Greene is sufficiently Roman Catholic to reject any non-incarnational view of divine love. Yet how is this to be shown, when human love is also seen, in an extreme Protestant mode, as merely one more deceptive form of the pride of self, one more sign of false consciousness and bad faith? In any final analysis, the issue is incapable of adequate resolution: all the novels can hope to do is to suggest the presence of charity in particular men and women while simultaneously protecting them from a pharisaic awareness of their own better feelings.

But this can be done only by convicting the protagonist of a curious lack of self-knowledge, or simply by obscuring vital evidence. The case of the priest in *The Power and the Glory* is again relevant: why does the giggling, frightened, self-doubting renegade risk death by refusing to join his fellow-clerics in their flight from the country? The question of motivation is not convincingly established:

> 'That's another thing I don't understand,' the lieutenant said, 'why you—of all people—should have stayed when the others ran.'
> 'They didn't all run,' the priest said.
> 'But why did you stay?'
> 'Once,' the priest said, 'I asked myself that. The fact is, a man isn't presented suddenly with two courses to follow: one good and one bad. He gets caught up. The first year—well, I didn't believe there was really any cause to run. Churches have been burnt before now. You know how often. It doesn't mean much. I thought I'd stay till next month, say, and see if things were better. Then—oh, you don't know how time can slip by. . . . Do you know I suddenly realised that I was the only priest left for miles around? There was one priest in particular—he had always disapproved of me. I have a tongue, you know, and it used to wag. He said—quite rightly—that I wasn't a firm character. He escaped. It felt—you'll laugh at this—just as it did at school when a bully I had been afraid of—for years—got too old for any more teaching and was turned out. . . .
> 'It was when he left I began to go to pieces. One thing went after another. I got careless about my duties. I began to drink. It would have been much better, I think, if I had gone too. Because pride was at work all the time. Not love of God. . . . I thought I was a fine fellow to have stayed when the others had gone. . . . I wasn't any use, but I stayed. At least, not much use. . . . It's a mistake one makes—to think just because a thing is difficult or dangerous. . . .' He made a flapping motion with his hands.

The priest has taken no definable moral decision: a man 'gets caught up', and then 'you don't know how time can slip by'; the vagueness of this is then concealed by a displacement of attention to the self-righteous fellow-priest who fled. That priest's flight throws the whisky priest himself into a morally favourable light, but also qualifies his courage: it was after that incident that he 'began to go to pieces', and one thing led, automatically, to another. The priest then settles on pride as his motive, and in doing so once more appeals to a moral condition which, given the lack of essential evidence, the reader can neither confirm nor effectively question. Because of his pride, he 'wasn't any use'; but that too explicitly demeaning comment is then instantly qualified: 'At least, not much use'. The priest's final comment trails off into inarticulate ambiguity: 'It's a mistake one makes—to think just because a thing is difficult or dangerous . . .'. If this is to be interpreted as hinting that the priest consciously embraced those dangers, judging his action more valuable on their account, then, even if this too is merely to be dismissed as proud self-deception, it seems difficult to square its suggestion of conscious courage with the notion that he has simply been 'caught up'.

If the whisky priest was merely 'caught up', the same can be said of Scobie. Scobie's inability actively to control his environment, to prevent the inexorable spreading of evil through the air breathed by innocents, is offered as part of the nature of things, a defeatism nurtured by the 'conditions of life'; but it also allows him to be led passively into a possibly heroic posture, by the sheer logic of his unheroically fragmented situation-ethics. Scobie, too, gets 'caught up', and like the whisky priest what he gets caught up in is a kind of sanctity which transcends pragmatism. It is important for the novel both to affirm the quality of virtue—to show it as more than mere circumstantial determinism—and yet to stress at the same time the seemingly inexorable, partial, piecemeal process by which it is attained, so as to avoid any damagingly pharisaic implication that it was a course of action he ever consciously chose. A kind of self-sacrifice possible only to the morally courageous must be endorsed, but not at the cost of questioning the wisdom of a pragmatic passivity. Once again, the novel has to tread an awkwardly narrow line between conscious and confused motivations, between the objective reality of goodness and a subjective unawareness of its presence. Scobie's impotent passivity, his chronic incapacity for decisive moral action, is a criticism of his behaviour; yet it is lessened in force, not only because the mood and comment of the novel co-operate in confirming

the intelligence of this stance (even the climate is made to suggest its natural inevitability: 'This isn't a climate for emotion
. . . anything like hate or love drives a man off his head'), but
because it is precisely his passivity, his desperately pragmatic
scepticism, which leads him to a courageous act and at the
same time shields him from any destructive belief in its value.
Because Scobie is caught up by his very pragmatism into an
action which both transcends that process and yet is also its
last, logical step, the novel is able to validate and criticise this
ethic at the same time. He is led, by decent, 'rational' behaviour,
to a kind of courage which outstrips the behaviour of the
decent rationalist.

A similar ambiguity is apparent in *The End of the Affair*; in
this novel, however, it is built into the very structure of the
work. The novel operates essentially at two distinct levels: on
one level we are shown the conscious motives and actions of
the characters; on a deeper level, the mysteriously obscure purposes which they are fulfilling, unknown to themselves, as the
agents of God's devious love. In this way, Greene is able to
provide himself with a structural framework for resolving the
disparities of human self-estimation and the reality of the divine
love at work within and between men. Because the action of
God is now an unconscious process, insidiously and invisibly
at work, the difficulties of accommodating the power of this
love to corrupt human motive and behaviour are lessened;
Sarah, Bendrix, Henry, Parkis and more minor characters can
act consciously at one level while the true 'meaning' of their
behaviour is revealed only within a deeper dimension of which
they are all for the most part unaware. In this way, Sarah's
dramatic conversion may be squared with her previous agnosti-
cism because it is an event for which she is really in no sense
fully responsible; we are asked to believe that it is the organic
culmination of that invisible process which began, unknown
to herself, with her secret baptism as a child. Because Sarah is
not fully responsible for her own holiness, she can be given
moral value without this qualifying her own judgement on

herself as 'a bitch and a fake'; the two levels, divine and human, can co-exist without mutual interference, and one distinct advantage of this is that Greene is thereby able to preserve his thesis that common human life is sterile and corrupt. Yet at the same time the action of grace cannot be shown as wholly deterministic and invisibly disembodied, for this would be to equate Sarah the saint with Bendrix and Smythe the rationalists. Somehow, the two levels of meaning must interact—Sarah must be shown, as a person, to have the qualities of God's love —without one level being fully reconciled to the other, since this would suggest that men were of their own efforts capable of merit—a thesis the novel wants to reject. So once more there is a problem: we can neither believe, nor disbelieve, Sarah's judgement of herself. To believe it is to dislocate too radically the action of grace and the quality of persons: to render Sarah morally equal to Bendrix. But to disbelieve it is to suggest that the love of God can issue in outstanding human value—can actively redeem, at least in a local sense, that fallenness which for Greene is 'given' from the outset. The ambiguity is 'resolved', as it was in *The Power and the Glory*, by the tactic of concealing essential evidence. Sarah, much more than the whisky priest, is presented to us obliquely, by virtue of the novel's structure: she is seen either from the tendentious angle of Bendrix's own tortured account, or through her own self-demeaning record in her diary. In neither case is she seen 'objectively'. What we *see* would suggest that her low self-estimation springs from the deceptions of humility; yet, as with the whisky priest, it is vital, if we are not to miss the tension between human cheapness and divine power, that we do not entirely dismiss it as such.

There is a parallel obscurity in the question of Sarah's vow to a God in whom, at the time, she has no conscious belief. 'Why did this promise stay,' she asks herself, 'like an ugly vase a friend has given and one waits for a maid to break it . . . ?' Sarah's own irritated bewilderment suggests an answer: it stayed because God wanted it to, against the grain of Sarah's own frustrated bitterness at the loss of Bendrix's love which was its result. Yet although responsibility for the persistence of the vow is to that extent removed from Sarah's own control, and any dangerous hint of consciously heroic love thereby avoided, it is not wholly that: for Sarah's commitment to her promise, against her own deepest instincts, *is* offered, elsewhere, as a distinguishing mark of personal sanctity. It is neither simply a question of a courageous decision which elevates her morally above others, nor simply a choice made for her by God himself: by sustaining this ambiguity, the novel refuses to choose clearly between seeing Sarah merely as the determined instrument of grace, or seeing her as a self-determining saint. Either alternative, in itself, would be detrimental to Greene's viewpoint. Thus, it is important that Sarah's death should be markedly unheroic—it results from her catching cold —yet it is also important that the cold should be caught in her efforts to avoid Bendrix, and so the temptation to betray God. Her death can neither be consciously chosen nor merely accidental: she must be protected alike from the falsities of both Christian martyrdom and sheerly human contingency. Once more, the possibility of outstanding virtue must be affirmed in the context of a radical suspicion of conscious goodness.

In a later novel, *A Burnt-Out Case*, the clash between 'heroism' and 'anti-heroism' becomes a dominant theme. Querry, the burnt-out architect, is cynically aware of his own worthlessness; yet his actions trigger off a conspiracy to enshrine him as a saint. The chief actions which lead us to be suspicious of his own radical self-disgust are his care of the injured African Deo Gratias, and his concern for the vulnerably innocent, maltreated Marie Rycker. Here is the incident where he follows Deo Gratias into the forest, vaguely aware that he may have met with an accident:

> His own presence here was hardly more explicable than that of Deo Gratias. The thought of his servant lying injured in the forest waiting for the call or footstep of any human being would perhaps at an earlier time have vexed him all night until

he was forced into making a token gesture. But now that he cared for nothing, perhaps he was being driven only by a vestige of intellectual curiosity. What had brought Deo Gratias here out of the safety and familiarity of the leproserie? . . . What was the meaning of the sweat he had seen pouring down the man's face? . . . Interest began to move painfully in him like a nerve that had been frozen. He had lived with inertia so long that he examined his 'interest' with clinical detachment. . . .

At the end of the path into the forest, Querry finds the African injured and paralysed with fright:

> After ten minutes of struggle Querry managed to drag his limbs out of the water—it was all he could do. . . . The fingerless hand fell on Querry's arm like a hammer and held him there.
> There was nothing to be done but wait for the morning. . . . He took Deo Gratias' hand to reassure him. . . . Deo Gratias grunted twice, and then uttered a word. It sounded like 'Pendélé'. . . .

Querry's motives for pursuing his servant are 'inexplicable'; or, if a motive is demanded, it is 'perhaps' merely curiosity. Yet that curiosity, while possibly 'clinical', is itself obscurely related to what the novel sees as best in Querry: his persistent search, despite the conscious detachment, for the path which leads to 'Pendélé', to a mysterious haven of peace. So while his concern for Deo Gratias is at one level an intellectual interest which is not allowed to count in his favour, the African's curious disappearance stirs in him, at a deeper level, that yearning for an absolute reality which renders him in some senses morally superior to those more committed rationalists or pragmatists who discount such strivings—Dr Colin, or the Father Superior. The decision to seek out Deo Gratias is 'inexplicable' rather than clearly defined; and once this is taken, Querry is passively caught up in an act of charity, led on by his own half-conscious motive to the point where 'There was nothing to be done but wait for the morning'. That 'nothing to be done' qualifies any hint of compassion by suggesting a circumstantial inevitability; yet the same comment cannot adequately explain his taking hold of the leper's hand to comfort him. One is forced to conclude that the novel is using here, rather less emphatically, something of the technique of *The End of the Affair*. Like Sarah, Querry's deepest motive is a search for God, but its very unconsciousness prevents him from being in possession of his own experience and so running the contaminating risks of valuing himself highly. Yet again, as in *The End of the Affair*, the meritorious motive cannot be allowed to remain wholly submerged: if it is to be more than mere determinism, it must find tangible expression at some point in the character's actual behaviour. And so the novel shows Querry perform a charitable act without, however, revealing his attitude: the account is kept scrupulously external. In a similar way, Querry's involvement with Marie Rycker appears to indicate in him a kind of negative humanity—it is chiefly through Querry's eyes that her brutally egoistic husband is exposed for what he is—yet once more the involvement which leads to the night in the hotel and so to Querry's death simply 'happens' as an accumulation of trivial actions, a process within which no isolatable moment of commitment occurs. The balance, as usual, is precariously preserved: Querry's comments on the sterility of the Ryckers' marriage count to underscore his cynical view of man; yet they also count, at least in a negative sense, to reveal in him a moral sensitivity and insight. Again, Querry's journey to the leper-hospital is a conscious renunciation of humanity; yet he is anxious from the beginning to help with menial tasks, and the discrepancy of motive is not successfully accounted for. Once more, we cannot explain the incongruency by saying that Querry is merely self-deceived, for this would be finally to invalidate a misanthropy which the novel wishes at least in part to endorse, and to slip into the camp of those who wish to make Querry a cult-hero and destroy him in the process; but on the other hand, we are meant to see, as with Scobie and the whisky priest, that the very stringency of his self-condemnation discloses a negative moral value:

He thought: there was only one thing I could do and that is reason enough for being here. I can promise you. Marie, *toute à toi*, all of you, never again from boredom or vanity to involve another human being in my lack of love. I shall do no more harm. . . .

This both emphasises the deceptions of human feeling, and by the same token reveals a sort of humanity in Querry. The novel is able to reconcile its affirmation and rejection of human love by suggesting that affirmative qualities must be implicit in such a rejection. In a parallel way, the book also implies that there is value present in the very unflinching honesty with which Querry confronts his own worthlessness: it is his honesty, after all, which distinguishes his own 'dark night of the soul' from Rycker's. To assert this is to lend Querry dignity without questioning his low self-estimation: in this novel, Greene can reconcile his paradox of a man being at once worthless and better than he thinks by finding his best qualities in the way he faces his worthlessness. The bad Catholic is redeemed by the very intensity of his scruples: 'You must have had a lot of belief once to miss it the way you do,' Colin tells Querry. It is no longer a case, as it was with Scobie and the whisky priest, that Querry is especially self-deceived: it is true, as the novel shows us, that he has little or no capacity for genuine love. Nevertheless, the man who continues to seek faith has already found it: once again value lies in good intentions, however obscure to consciousness. Querry shares the pragmatic rationalism of Dr Colin, against the pious egoism of Rycker or Father Thomas; yet his quest for an absolute value beyond the mess of human reality also lends him a certain superiority to the rationalists. He shares the Superior's lack of concern with moral theology, but also, in a way hardly evident to himself, Father Thomas's preoccupation with absolute questions; they are both, as Colin comments, 'men of extremes', whereas Colin himself—the most positively admirable character in the novel —is not. Querry is thus protected from being completely identified either with materialistic rationalism or metaphysical dogmatism, with a conscious commitment to the human world or with an egoistic asceticism which rejects it. In the case of Querry, as of Scobie, Greene is able to have his pragmatic scepticism and reach beyond it at the same time.

It is worth turning at this point to *The Quiet American*. The book centres on a conflict, common to Greene's writing, between the destructive ruthlessness of innocence and principled action on the one hand, and the corrupting guilt of pragmatic humanism on the other. Pyle, the quiet American, is strong, innocent, decisive and so dangerous; Fowler is weak, cynical, compromised and corrupted, and so both inferior and superior to Pyle's kind of virtue. Like the priest of *The Power and the Glory*, Fowler opposes decisively radical social action; he does so in the name of a desire to preserve life which, like the priest's, is based on a belief in the unchanging meanness of human nature—a belief which Pyle is unable to challenge because it is founded on Fowler's 'experience', as against the rigidities of his own 'ideology'. (The radically ideological nature of the stance to which Fowler's experience has led him is not, of course, allowed.) It is important that Fowler's jaundiced view of the human situation should not go uncriticised—indeed, as often with Greene, it is part of the quality of that view that its exponent should be self-critical. Fowler can see that Pyle is in many ways the 'better' man, and so can we; indeed, given a wholly different context, there is in the relationship of Fowler and Pyle a faint but detectable resonance of the relationship of Pinkie and Rose in *Brighton Rock*. In both cases, the role of the innocent partner is unwittingly to reveal to the other his own corruption. But Fowler's self-disgust lends credence to his condemnation of Pyle at the same time as it permits him to acknowledge his inferiority: the self-disgust springs from the same depth of 'experience' from which the criticism of Pyle's murderously naïve ideologising is launched. And because Fowler is empty of self-esteem, his dislike of Pyle can be seen as disinterested. In a better world, Pyle's energy and commitment would overshadow Fowler's flaccid cynicism, and to this extent Fowler is critically placed; but because Fowler's view that a better world is impossible is, despite the criticism, endorsed, Pyle can be rejected. (He is, in any case, something of a straw target, with his crew-cut and volumes of ideology; the effective humour reaped at his expense comes suspiciously easily.) The man who rates human potential highly is thus destructive; the man with a confused regard for life has a low estimation of its worth.

Yet once more Greene faces an intractable problem. If the rejection of Pyle's murderous innocence is to have validity, it must be made from a humane standpoint; yet what is being denied is in fact the view that significant human value exists. Fowler, then, must be allowed a certain humanity—enough, in fact, to let him conquer Pyle in ideological argument without convicting him of ideological views, and so of an articulate commitment to purposive action. Thus, when the two men are arguing in the watch-tower, Fowler can clinch the political discussion by commenting: 'I've been here a long time. You know, it's lucky I'm not *engagé*, because there are things I might be tempted to do—because here in the East—well, I don't like Ike. I like—well, these two.' 'These two' are the silent Vietnamese soldiers who crouch with them in the tower; and Fowler's appeal to them is meant to undercut the 'unreal' ideologising to the level of the simply human. 'I'd like those two poor buggers there to be happy—that's all.' He appeals to a life in which the Vietnamese peasants can simply get enough rice and avoid being shot at: 'They want one day to be much the same as another'.

Fowler's political position is, in fact, deeply confused. The question of how peace and enough rice are to be attained— the fact that it is, inescapably, a *political* question, and that it slides over certain additional issues, such as whether the peasants are to govern themselves or be governed by imperialist regimes—is seriously blurred. Fowler is, of course, rabidly anti-American, but to avoid the disruptions of 'ideology' he must launch his satirical assault on U.S. imperialism from a non-political standpoint: from a commitment to 'the human' which detaches it from its inevitably political embodiments, and which moreover must avoid imbuing 'the human' itself with too much value. This is the point of his suggestion that the peasants merely want enough rice and a settled routine: to imply a sympathy with the peasant which at the same time contains the judgement that he lacks the capacity to see further than his stomach. Yet there is a further, more serious ambiguity in Fowler's attitude: the conflict between his passionate anti-Americanism and his carefully nurtured cult of dispassionately objective *dégagement*. The first would indicate a humane indignation; the second implies its opposite. The problem of resolving these attitudes is lessened to some degree by the fact that Fowler's anti-Americanism is for the most part less an objection to what the Americans *do*—and so, at least by implication, a commitment to their victims—than a criticism of what they *are*, an almost physical disgust for the trivia of hairstyle and manner. Fowler's anti-Americanism is closer to a vulgar snobbery than to a shrewd analysis of the brutalities of U.S. imperialism, a fact which the novel itself seems significantly not to question. Nevertheless, Fowler's anti-American feeling draws him emotionally towards an engagement he would intellectually repudiate: if he were not *dégagé*, there are things he 'might be tempted to do', morally committed courses of action he might follow. These would be 'temptation', since committed action is bound to fail and destroy: one of the novel's epigraphs is Arthur Clough's comment that 'I do not like being moved: for the will is excited; and action is a most dangerous thing'. Yet such tempting actions might also reveal a kind of moral fibre: they would have behind them the ratifying force of Fowler's 'best self', his disgust at imperialist manipulation.

The climax of the novel is Fowler's submission to temptation. Swayed by a 'moment of emotion', a swift response of shocked horror at the bomb-murders with which Pyle is involved, he betrays the American to his death. Again, there is no clearly defined moment of moral decision: having decided to have Pyle silenced, he gives him various chances to escape. Yet in taking this action, Fowler is obedient to the impulse of common humanity he felt for the soldiers in the tower: his detachment is exposed as self-deception and yields to principled decision. To the extent that his action emerges from the humanism which gives him a title to reject Pyle, it is related to what is most morally valuable in him: by performing it, he transcends his sterile cynicism and betrays a feeling for life. Yet to the extent to which the act of consigning Pyle to his death reaches beyond the confusions and half-commitments of pragmatism into serious involvement, it must fall under the strictures which Fowler himself has made on Pyle. Thus Fowler's action both substantiates a humanity which is, in the last analysis, more worthy than Pyle's fanaticism, and at the same time, through Fowler's guilt at having killed a kind and honourable man, serves to ratify the wisdom of his previous detachment. Both involvement and detachment are therefore criticised; but the 'moral' is not quite that detachment is desirable, but impossible. Detachment is desirable, but only to the degree that it does not sterilise the humane feelings by which criticism of others' more committed (and so more destructive) involvements can be made. The uncommitted man must be shown as both inhumanly cynical and humanly sensitive: either perspective can be selected to attack the revolutionary, but both are necessary if the attack is to rest on a version of man both inferior and superior to the revolutionary's own. And this, essentially, is what Greene's novels want to do.

II

It is possible to express the tensions we have traced within Greene's work in slightly different terms. There is a sense in which the ethics of Greene's 'bad' Catholic characters differ from the ethics of pragmatic humanism only in the guilt by which the actions they lead to are accompanied. Yet the guilt is an essential element: as we have seen, it allows humanism to be both qualified and endorsed. Greene's kind of Christianity, in fact, makes remarkably little difference to the quality of human life itself: it makes its difference felt chiefly at the end of life, in the reality of death. God is peace and love, the Pendélé at the end of the path through the decayed human jungle, glimpsed in frustrating moments through its undergrowth; in *The End of the Affair*, God is the presence which emerges when human relationships have broken down. Neither Bendrix nor Fowler are Christians, and the fact has some significance: because of it, Greene can distance himself to some extent from their crude acquisitiveness. Yet what is striking is how little difference belief would really make to either man's attitudes. Fowler himself defines what faith might mean to him in a way which suggests this fact: 'The job of a reporter is to expose and record. I had never in my career discovered the inexplicable. . . . I had no visions or miracles in my repertoire of memories.' Christianity is seen as the 'inexplicable', which makes a difference to ordinary human life chiefly by not fitting in with it— by being superadded vision and miracle. And in this sense, it need not alter the sceptical version of man which Bendrix and Fowler hold. Through these men, Greene does not simply express a view of what the world seems like without God; he expresses what the world seems like with God too. It is just that, for Sarah and Deo Gratias, there is something beyond the world which the atheist does not recognise. Greene's attitude in this respect seems, indeed, to have become increasingly pessimistic as he has developed: it is true that divine grace makes a qualitative difference to the whisky priest's behaviour in *The Power and the Glory*, and still, although less true, in the case of Scobie; but in Sarah's case, the symbols of divine love are miracles which occur after her death. She is, so to speak, most effectively present in the world after she has left it.

There is a theological basis to this way of seeing. Although Greene's novels centre again and again on the truths of passion and crucifixion, the definitive event of Christian faith—resurrection—finds no place in their economy. God is not seen as the living power which sustains and renews human relationship; He is what is found among the debris of their collapse. We can return at this point to a problem touched on earlier: the tension between Greene's extreme Protestant view of men as radically corrupt, and his more orthodox belief in a divine love which is somehow tangibly incarnated. The novels escape this dilemma by seeing God as incarnate, not in human creativity, but in human failure. Failure, for Greene, is at once what is most essentially human about man (Scobie speaks of 'the loyalty we all feel to unhappiness—the sense that that is where we really belong') and yet is also what reveals him in the least heroic or impressive light. It is therefore safe to love failure, as Sarah 'loves' the disfigured Smythe, because it involves one in loving, not humanity, but its negation—in loving that in man which finally points beyond him. 'I am kissing pain,' says Sarah when she presses her lips to Smythe's strawberry-mark, 'and pain belongs to You as happiness never does.' The more men are exposed as broken and corrupted failures, the more one can love them and so have one's 'humanism', but the more, by the same token, they endorse an anti-humanist view of their fallenness. The more you love men, the less you value them: 'Here,' says Scobie, 'you could love human beings nearly as God loved them, knowing the worst'. When the whisky priest ponders that 'it needed a god to die for the half-hearted and the corrupt', he dignifies and demeans humanity at the same time. In the light of this, the humility of Greene's characters gains an added significance: what the novels do not see is that their characters' inability to value themselves is intimately related to their inability to value others. Their attitude is the direct reverse of the traditional Christian insight that, in order to be able genuinely to love another, one must also be able to love oneself.

The whisky priest's sense of solidarity with suffering, guilt and weakness is one instance of a pervasive belief, in almost all of Greene's novels, that it is here that God is most concretely present. It is only by the experience of suffering, guilt, weakness, and so of compassion, that the pharisaic egoisms of respectalbe religion, hygienic innocence and the ethic of success can be avoided. Yet this, while radical in its attitude towards orthodoxy ('God might forgive cowardice and passion, but was it possible to forgive the habit of piety?'), is at another point deeply conservative: it leads the whisky priest to a rejection of those beliefs which would hope to remove the unhappiness where men 'really belong'. Once men cannot be pitied they cannot be loved, since the love was, all along, only a form of pity. Scobie wants his wife Louise to be happy, but can't love success: 'He thought: it was the hysterical woman who felt the world laughing behind her back that I loved. I love failure: I can't love success. And how successful she looks, sitting there: one of the saved. . . .' The extent to which pity degrades its object (the term is apt) is realised: it occurs to Scobie that Louise is 'someone of human stature with her own sense of responsibility, not simply the object of his care and kindness'. He half-recognises that, precisely because his 'automatic terrible pity' goes out to *any* human need, regardless of the particular person involved, it is to that degree a kind of abstraction. Yet although the dangers of pity are seen, it is preferable, in the end, to the callow arrogance of love.

Greene's novels, then, have to accommodate their strong impulse towards a rejection of human experience itself as inherently flawed—the instinct of the police lieutenant, who wishes to 'destroy everything' and begin afresh—to a tired respect for a pragmatic negotiation of ordinary life. It is worth looking finally at one of Greene's earliest novels, *Brighton Rock*, since there some of the tensions we have discussed seem least satisfactorily resolved. The evil of Pinkie, in *Brighton Rock*, lies in his uncompromisingly total rejection of ordinary human reality: of the texture of human experience itself. His evil is closely linked with his social and sexual ignorance: he embodies a kind of pure negation, an 'annihilating eternity'. Yet Pinkie's view of experience is time and again confirmed by the novel itself: his revolted rejection of life is underpinned by the book's mood and imagery, which remorselessly elaborate the selective sordidities of Brighton to the status of an entire human condition:

'The sun slid off the sea and like a cuttlefish shot into the sky with the stain of agonies and endurances'. Brighton, a seedy, flashy, candy-floss world, is seen by the novel with a coldly dehumanising perception which parallels Pinkie's own responses. 'Down the steps of the Cosmopolitan came a couple of expensive women with bright brass hair and ermine coats and heads close together like parrots exchanging metallic confidences . . . they flashed their pointed painted nails at each other and cackled.' 'Bright', 'brass', 'metallic', 'flashed', 'painted', 'cackled': these are the terms in which the whole of Brighton is seen, and the verbal artifice, the over-insistent, over-written dragooning of casual detail into tendentious effect, is characteristic of the whole book. The Brighton world finds its unreal epitome in Ida Arnold, the brassily sentimental whore who intervenes to save the innocent Rose from the evil Pinkie:

> 'You leave her alone,' the woman said. 'I know all about you.' It was as if she were in a strange country: the typical Englishwoman abroad. She hadn't even got a phrasebook. She was as far from either of them as she was from Hell—or Heaven. Good and evil lived in the same country, spoke the same language, came together like old friends, feeling the same completion, touching hands beside the iron bedstead.

Ida enters the metaphysical world of Pinkie and Rose as a self-righteous day-tripper from the land of pragmatic humanism; for all her knowledge of 'human nature' she is a vulgar and irrelevant voice in the absolutist country into which she blunders. Pinkie and Rose belong to a metaphysical élite who have transcended the seedy ethics of quotidian experience for the superior world of those 'real' enough to embrace or reject divine salvation. 'She!' says Pinkie of Ida. 'She's just nothing'; and the novel confirms his judgement.

Pinkie, then, is damned because of his incapacity to surrender himself to life; yet we are nowhere shown that life as particularly worth surrendering to. We condemn his murders, of course, but not from any standpoint of sympathy with his brutal or broken victims. If Ida Arnold and Pinkie's underworld friends are truly representative of the human condition, then it is difficult to avoid feeling that Pinkie is damned by his author for holding a view of life which the novel validates.

At least, this would be so if it were not for Rose, Pinkie's innocent girl. Rose is the mute, living embodiment of the terrible judgement in store for Pinkie, accompanying him everywhere, inseparable from his nature; it is Rose who incarnates that capacity for loving self-abandonment which manifests Pinkie as lost. Rose is the criterion by which Pinkie is damned, yet at least two facts in the novel work against the effectiveness of this. First, Rose's goodness is entirely passive: it cannot assume the form of positive action, for positive action belongs to the self-righteously ethical world of Ida Arnold, the realm of obtusely interfering do-gooding. Action, in any case, presumes a knowledge of the world which the incorruptible Rose cannot be allowed. Rose is the only person in the world who symbolises the love which Pinkie has denied, but she is hardly 'in' the world at all: she belongs to Brighton no more than Pinkie. (It is significant, incidentally, that Brighton is where Pinkie grew up: by making his home a no-home, a seaside resort for London, a town usually thought of as a place people visit rather than inhabit, the novel detaches him from any natural locality and so renders his evil less environmentally explicable.) Secondly, Rose's association with Pinkie works as much in his favour as to his disadvantage: they are linked together as the complementary polarities of good and evil, and the differences between them are less significant, for both of them, than their mutual opposition to the shabbily unheroic world of Ida Arnold. Rose recognises what Pinkie is, in a world too flashily one-dimensional to evaluate the terrifying meaning of his life; Pinkie, unlike other Greene characters, is fully aware of his own metaphysical significance, and it is a criticism of the world that it cannot see this significance. Pinkie may be 'evil', but he is not 'corrupt': his evil is a pure, pristine integrity, a priestly asceticism which refuses the contaminations of ordinary living. Moreover, in this early novel, the disgusted desire to shake oneself free from experience is not emphasised as naïvety or false consciousness; the incidents which reveal Pinkie's un-worldly integrity of evil—his sexual clumsiness with the girl in the car-park, for instance—count at least as much against social 'decadence' as against Pinkie himself. Pinkie *is* innocent, but while he is damned for it, it is also a mark of his superiority to the Ida Arnolds of the world. His innocence is not a fault which could be corrected with time, as one could argue, per-haps, about Pyle in *The Quiet American*: it is integral to what he is, part of the essence of his evil. And to that degree it is part of his general, metaphysical superiority to the Brighton world. Pinkie cannot understand human reality, but the human reality we are shown has nothing substantial about it to be understood; Pinkie and Brighton are two negations linked in a fixed opposition. Pinkie regards human involvement as des-picable weakness, and is damned for it; yet the novel's major image of such involvement is the despicable Ida.

Brighton Rock, then, has its share of the ambiguities we have seen elsewhere in Greene, but it also has its divergencies. By choosing a wholly evil figure as its focus, the book can indulge that vision of the world as putrid corruption which is a signi-ficant element of other novels without this leading to difficult tensions with a simultaneous suggestion of virtue. Virtue is affirmed elsewhere, in Rose; yet in a way which, as we have seen, connives at rather than qualifies the detailed imagery of fallenness. Again, by choosing an evil 'hero' (and the term has, perhaps, some force), the novel is saved from later problems of accommodating conscious to unconscious motives. If it is of the essence of good for Greene that it should be to some degree humbly ignorant of itself, it is of the essence of evil that it should know itself for what it is: a man cannot be damned against his will.

As a consequence of this difference in the protagonist, there is a corresponding difference in the attitude towards corrup-tion. The 'good' men of Greene's later novels cannot take

Pinkie's uncompromising stance towards the ordinary universe, although they are constantly attracted to some version of it; to do this would be to betray their goodness, which lies, precisely, in a solidarity with human weakness. What is interesting in *Brighton Rock*, in this respect, is the ambiguous characterisation of Ida Arnold; for Ida is both a warm, relaxed, lenient earth-mother, embracing all human weakness to her ample bosom, and yet, in her pursuit of Pinkie and Rose, a relentless avenger of wrong. The novel, in fact, has some difficulty in squaring these disparate aspects of Ida: in endowing her at once with a breezy hedonism and an adequate motivation in her remorseless quest for justice. The aesthetic weakness embodies a moral dilemma: it springs from the novel's desire to reveal ordinary life not only as corrupt, but also as crassly assertive and interfering, and so to engage it in a confrontation with metaphysics which will expose its inferiority. The attempt is unconvincing: it entails our belief in Ida as both amoral vitalist and indignant moralist. The novel, once more, is over-insistent: it is torn between an impulse to dismiss routine life as glitteringly empty, and a need to worst it in argument.

In Greene's next important novel, *The Power and the Glory*, the situation has significantly changed: corruption and self-righteousness are no longer clumsily combined within the same person, but confront each other as polarities. This is the condition we have examined throughout, with its attendant problems and ambivalences. The exploration of evil in *Brighton Rock* is in one sense a dead-end; Greene turns from it to a more subtle and shaded analysis, in which despair and virtue, value and cheapness, are intricately interwoven. One condition for doing this is the transplanting of the action outside England, to the tropics: for here a corruption which in the domestic setting of *Brighton Rock* is seen merely as flashily or brutally superficial becomes full-blooded and intense. Deaths, betrayals and despair are now no longer confined to a criminal underworld within the 'sordid' respectabilities of a seaside resort, but become the fabric of a whole way of life. And so a different attitude may be taken to the 'fallen' world: whereas the official world of Brighton is merely seedy, the worlds of Africa, Latin America and the East are seen as both seedy and extreme, decrepit and exotic. And because corruption is more exotic and intense, it can be connected with the imagery of redemption and damnation which in *Brighton Rock* was jealously confined to an élite. The half-caste of *The Power and the Glory* can be related to metaphysical conditions in a way impossible for Ida Arnold. In these situations, as we have seen, Greene is able to find in the realities of suffering and weakness a value absent in the earlier novel: by the dialectics of death and salvation, cynicism and heroism, meanness and moral worth, a compassionate engagement with those merely despised in *Brighton Rock* can be made to consort with a rejection of the human world, and of the possibilities of sanctity within it, which still owes much to Pinkie's way of seeing.

III

The relation between Green and Orwell is not, at first sight, an obvious one: yet I have tried in this chapter to discuss the world of Greene's novels in terms which enforce significant connections with what has been said of Orwell. Like Orwell, Greene projects a seedy and hopeless world, a pervasive corruption which is both disgusting and yet—when compared with the pieties of privileged conservatism or the dreams of revolution—solidly 'real'. Like Orwell, too, Greene criticises both the formulations of radical ideology and the falsity of *dégagement*: both writers remain desperately bound to a quotidian world which is hated but which cannot be changed. Greene has available, of course, a 'totalisation' of a kind denied to Orwell: that of Roman Catholic orthodoxy. That orthodoxy can provide a way of transcending the pressures of routine experience, but only partially: the only way to achieve such transcendence is to remain wryly committed to the entangling morass of 'fallen' human life. A totalisation exists, but it can be lived only negatively, as a revelation of human inadequacies; a salvation which transcends the world is possible, but the world is not changed by it. In all these ways, Greene the 'metaphysical' novelist is more deeply influenced by the pressures and limits of a particular social world than the novels would have us believe; in feeling and attitude, he is closer to Orwell, and to a specific strain in the English novel, than to the more overtly theological writers with whom he is often compared. The 'annihilating' eyes of Pinkie may embody an eternity beyond the limits of specific place and time: but the expressions which that 'eternity' is given, as, indeed, with all Greene's theological values, are more deeply determined by a particular cultural standpoint than Greene is prepared to admit.

CHAPTER V

T. S. Eliot and the Uses of Myth

I

IN previous chapters I have traced a range of problems through the work of some English novelists: and these problems have hinged on the common difficulty of discovering, in a social condition felt as fragmentary and flawed, a vantage-point from which a coherent moral and artistic statement could be made. Conrad the expatriate, Waugh the upper-class observer, Orwell the social critic, Greene the Catholic metaphysician, are all in various ways exiles within a society; they have in common a recognition of certain limitations within their culture which drives them to search for a point of transcendence from which it can be criticised and placed. The dialectic involved in that exploration—the pattern of attraction and repulsion with which they confront the ordinary experience of their own immediate worlds—has been the subject of this inquiry; and to the extent that each writer can be seen as representative of a wider *genre* or literary attitude within contemporary literature, each has an added dimension of significance. Between them, I would claim, they offer a diagram of some of the major possible responses to English society in our century.

I have argued that none of the novels dealt with so far have been able fully to transcend certain limitations of their culture in order to articulate a total statement of it. But in the search for what I have called a 'totalisation', for a cohering standpoint, framework or symbolism by which a writer can surpass the immediate prejudices of his own partial experience to achieve a complete, impersonal and 'objective' version of reality in the image of nineteenth-century realism, one major mode has been predominant throughout the twentieth century: the mode of myth. In the work of Eliot, Joyce, Yeats and (to some extent) Lawrence, myth has again and again been offered as fulfilling the purposes which, in the work of the novelists we have examined already, could not be attained by a significant organisation of the structures of ordinary experience. Through the symbolic resources of myth, ways of eliciting, ordering and evaluating the inner structure of a culture have seemed available; and that availability has been gratefully put to use, in the absence of alternative forms of understanding. My intention in this chapter is to examine some of the uses of myth in the work of T. S. Eliot, both as a way of arriving at a critical estimation of Eliot's poetry, and as a way of commenting more generally on the value and viability of myth as an interpretative model by which literature can make sense of life.

II

The only way of expressing emotion in the form of art is by finding an 'objective correlative'; in other words, a set of objects, a situation, a chain of events which shall be the formula of that *particular* emotion; such that when the external facts, which must terminate in sensory experience, are given, the emotion is immediately invoked.

To achieve the 'objective correlative' within poetry—to fuse, in a precise congruency, subjective feeling with its objective formula—is in some sense to achieve the public impersonality of a 'totalisation'. When the uncertain, fluctuating complexities of private feeling can pass wholly into a stilled objectivity, into the focused calm of an exactly delineated sensory image, the result is the attainment, at a local or general level, of that desired relation between writer and reality which we have seen lacking in other authors. In the achieved moment of the objective correlative, according to Eliot's theory, the poet passes beyond the encapsulating limits of private, partial experience into an impersonally integrated objectivity, a coherence of understanding: the 'objective correlative' image must be taken together with Eliot's simile of the 'bit of finely filiated platinum' around which disparate fragments of reality crystallise into organic totality. Yet the poet does not on that account lose living relation with his own experience, overbalancing into blank neutrality. The dangerously subjectivist elements of his sensibility are transcended; but the formula through which they are surmounted, while in one sense 'objective', retains the grain and bias of a personal perception. We shall have more to say of this process later, in considering its relation to Eliot's use of myth; at present, it is necessary to trace the search for the objective correlative through some of Eliot's early poetry. The case I want to argue is that the relationship between the 'objective correlative' theory and the practice of Eliot's poetry must be seen essentially as one of trial and exploration: as *search*. In the early poems, the objective correlative, in a sense broader than the realisations of local imagery, is not achieved; or, to put it more exactly, the subject-matter of some of these early poems is itself the quest for the objective correlative.

The Love Song of J. Alfred Prufrock is the earliest, and clearest, example. Prufrock's search is for a formulation of his inherently confused and ambiguous feelings, a formulation at once desired and feared: on the one hand, the wry agony of 'It is impossible to say just what I mean!'; on the other hand, a dread of 'The eyes that fix you in a formulated phrase', that pin you, wriggling, to the wall. The objective correlative which the whole poem suggests is, precisely, the condition of being unable to arrive at one: Eliot gains complete and significant expression via Prufrock's comic inability to do so. It is worth noticing, however, that Prufrock's problem is not only that of connecting known feeling to its objective formula: it is the problem of knowing, for lack of that formula, precisely what the feeling is at all. In this sense the poem interestingly exposes the epistemological flaw in Eliot's own theory: the belief that 'private' feeling can in some sense pre-exist, or be identified apart from, its particular public embodiments. Throughout the poem, Prufrock edges, crab-like, towards an elusive central utterance which is no sooner touched on than retracted; and this neurotic ebb and flow of consciousness, this rhythm of probing and withdrawal, is related to the epistemological ambivalence of the 'objective correlative' theory. Is it that Prufrock has, indeed, some important proposal to make which is withdrawn in the face of an obtusely uncomprehending society, or can the point of articulation never be reached because the feeling, given the lack of public categories of interpretation, appears to have a substance which is merely illusory? Is it, in fact, merely a surging negativity, an embodied nothing, a dream-like sensation empty in proportion to its inflated cosmic intensity? The first reading would register a satirical point against Prufrock's society, the second against himself: and the two satiric modes, here as elsewhere, are kept in finely ambiguous tension.

The uncertainty of this pattern of exposure and retraction registers itself most obviously in the poem's marked variations of evenness and intensity. The metrical pattern alternates between long, lurching, artlessly vulnerable lines, pedantically over-explicit yet slightly uncontrolled—

> *Let fall upon its back the soot that falls from chimneys. . . .*
> *And I have known the arms already, known them all. . . .*

—and short, stabbing or clinching lines, which assert a sort of control only at the cost of bathetic triteness. The poem opens with a clashing dissonance of both types of line, underlining their awkward dissimilarity by the ironic unity of rhyme:

> *Let us go then, you and I,*
> *When the evening is spread out against the sky . . .*

The poem is shot through with fussily repetitive devices, attempts at definition which merely display a nervous indeterminacy of over-emphasis, a wordy, mechanical fumbling which baulks the movement forwards in a sort of fidgeting displacement of energy:

> *The yellow fog that rubs its back upon the window-panes,*
> *The yellow smoke that rubs its muzzle on the window-panes . . .*

> *And indeed there will be time . . .*
> *There will be time, there will be time*
> *To prepare a face to meet the faces that you meet;*
> *There will be a time to murder and create. . . .*

There are equally significant variations of tone: the metaphor of fog-as-cat is roguishly playful, slackening the intensity of the first stanza's undertow of menace and culminating in a minor key of confident finality—

> *Slipped by the terrace, made a sudden leap,*
> *And seeing that it was a soft October night,*
> *Curled once about the house, and fell asleep*

—but the clinching rhyme is latently deceptive, luring the reader into a false sense of security ruffled by the dislocation of the bizarrely 'cohering' sensibility which yokes cat and fog together. Is the opening image of the evening as 'a patient etherised upon a table' to be read, in the light of this, as equally playful, or is it of more insidious intent? Are we meant to laugh at Prufrock, or to share his sense of disturbance in the face of an insidiously invading society? Again, there is a curious use of exclamation marks, casually, perhaps gratuitously heightening a tone—

> *Arms that are braceleted and white and bare*
> *(But in the lamplight, downed with light brown hair!)*

—or raising a potentially delusory confidence—

> *And the afternoon, the evening, sleeps so peacefully!*

In both cases, exclamation marks create a quality of feeling for which there is a disturbing lack of context: they suggest a subtle unhinging of object and response. Encompassing these local unevennesses is a pervasive variation of texture: stumbling, chloroformed lines are suddenly sharpened by transient *aperçus,* dramatic but ephemeral crystallisations of consciousness in material fragments—butt-ends, coffee spoons, transfixing pins

—which are always inert images: discrete physical objects marooned in a tremulous wash of consciousness.

Prufrock, to exploit Eliot's own simile, is the piece of platinum around which experience fails meaningfully to cohere. Objects in his world remain either atomically disparate— fetishised parts (gestures, skirts, arms, eyes) which intimate, but also occlude, a complete meaning—or can be interrelated, like the cat and fog, only by a dislocated cerebral permutation. The world is crammed with a heterogeneous collection of items, but the more vividly they present themselves to consciousness, the less possible it is to organise them significantly:

> . . . *After the sunsets and the dooryards and the sprinkled streets,*
> *After the novels, after the teacups, after the skirts that trail*
>   *along the floor—*
> *And this, and so much more?—*
> *It is impossible to say just what I mean!*

The more consciousness expands to comprehend these frag-ments, the more it confronts its own inflated emptiness; the more imprecise and unformulated it grows, the more elusively significant it seems to itself but the less, on that account, it can discover a satisfactory correlative. It is, finally, only 'the evening' which can vaguely imply an objective correlative for Prufrock's condition: and the comprehensiveness of that must be had at the cost of inexactness.

At only one point in the poem does Prufrock move, tenta-tively, towards an objective correlative of his experience:

> *Shall I say, I have gone at dusk through narrow streets*
> *And watched the smoke that rises from the pipes*
> *Of lonely men in shirt sleeves, leaning out of windows? . . .*

The momentary exposure is protected by the form of a ques-tion; and it is followed, typically, by a sharp retreat into a desired unconsciousness:

> *I should have been a pair of ragged claws*
> *Scuttling across the floors of silent seas.*

But the significance of the exposure is not only this: it is also that what we have, in the first quotation above, is really an objective correlative without its sustaining subjective feeling. We have the formula, but miss the attitude it is meant to crystal-lise; or, to use Eliot's own phrase in *The Dry Salvages*, 'we had the experience but missed the meaning'. So, on his nearest approach to an objective correlative of his emotion, Prufrock overbalances into blank externality. Throughout the poem, meanings and experience never precisely engage: for much of the time, social reality is too thin and fragmentary to bear the pressure of Prufrock's large but nebulous 'meanings'; but when a public formula is found, as above, the meanings it is supposed to incarnate merely dissolve, leaving only a faint residue of sense. It is significant, in the light of this, that the only place in the poem where attitude and object genuinely interlock into a statement at once personal and impersonal, lyrical and authori-tative, is a place where the objects in question belong, not to society, but to mythology:

> . . . *I have heard the mermaids singing, each to each.*
>
> *I do not think that they will sing to me.*
>
> *I have seen them riding seaward on the waves*
> *Combing the white hair of the waves blown back*
> *When the wind blows the water white and black.*
>
> *We have lingered in the chambers of the sea*
> *By sea-girls wreathed with seaweed red and brown*
> *Till human voices wake us, and we drown.*

Prufrock is in part, clearly enough, a satire on the society which inhibits its protagonist's self-expression; to this extent Prufrock himself is used to focus a criticism on his environ-ment. But that social satire is never really dominant as an ele-ment in the poem, since the 'society' which Prufrock shelters from and surveys hardly exists on its own public terms: it exists as a projection of his own responses, a facet of his troubled consciousness. On the one hand, his world is intensely solipsis-tic; but it is also present to him as an inertly material facticity which drives his feelings back on themselves into incoherence. Prufrock is fascinated by the world, by its arms and perfumes, but also bored by it: social reality is paradoxically both eccentrically disturbing and tediously over-familiar. In this sense he is both too separate, and not separate enough, from his experience to integrate it into articulate meaning: he is both too close to his own social existence to attain a critical, impersonal vantage-point outside it, and too estranged from living relation with his world to be himself much more than a symptom of its emptiness. The poem thus holds a fine balance between a satire of Prufrock and a criticism of his society. The satire directed at Prufrock himself is tempered to some degree by the criticism of others which he is able to make, and in that sense Prufrock gains a margin of superiority—even, in the closing lines, of dignified pathos—over his surroundings. On the other hand, as I have suggested, Prufrock is both too much, and too little, a part of the society for him to have any genuine title to criticise it: he is both too identified with its forms of feeling, and too alienated from its values, to discover the operative distance at which real criticism could strike home. Indeed, it is uncertain whether the generalising statement which he is able to make in the poem's final lines is really his at all: the speaking voice hovers indeterminately between the poet and his persona.

Portrait of a Lady offers both contrast and continuity with *Prufrock*. Continuity, in so far as the experience which the narrator describes is at one level not separable from his own consciousness; contrast, in that the fact of this projection now emerges into explicit and self-critical recognition. The emphasis of 'portrait' is significant: there is a manipulative aesthetic at work in the poem, moulding the recorded scene to the emotionally biased requirements of the narrator:

Among the smoke and fog of a December afternoon
You have the scene arrange itself—as it will seem to do—
With 'I have saved this afternoon for you';
And four wax candles in the darkened room,

Four rings of light upon the ceiling overhead,
An atmosphere of Juliet's tomb
Prepared for all the things to be said, or left unsaid.
We have been, let us say, to hear the latest Pole
Transmit the Preludes, through his hair and finger-tips.
'So intimate, this Chopin, that I think his soul
Should be resurrected only among friends
Some two or three, who will not touch the bloom
That is rubbed and questioned in the concert room.'
—And so the conversation slips
Among velleities and carefully caught regrets
Through attenuated tones of violins
Mingled with remote cornets
And begins.

'You have the scene arrange itself—as it will seem to do' is a self-consciously cavalier touch, remotely off-hand with the autonomous detail of the experience; and in the following lines, true to this beginning, that experience is stripped to a mere notation ('four wax candles . . . four rings of light . . .') and a cryptically generalising literary reference. 'We have been, *let us say*' again betrays the casually supercilious style, placing, patrician, remote: the reality of the concert is reduced by it to a quick sardonic sketch. In the final lines, a human conversation merges into an aesthetic construct of the poet's own: a distant blending of impersonal sounds supposedly elicited from, in fact projected on to, the human voices.

The point of the poem, of course, is that this bland confidence suffers *hubris*. The lady's conversation is a quiltwork of stale Romantic clichés, but it is enough, even so, to confront the poet with his own paralysis of response, and it is he who becomes the final target of the satire:

Well! and what if she should die some afternoon . . .
Should die and leave me sitting pen in hand
With the smoke coming down above the housetops . . .
Would she not have the advantage, after all?
This music is successful with a 'dying fall'

Now that we talk of dying—
And should I have the right to smile?

The poet is forced to confront the presumptiveness of his own aesthetic manipulations: unlike *Prufrock*, the social world is now seen to exist on its own, admittedly trivial, terms, as the ladies talking of Michelangelo in the first poem become, here, suddenly articulate and autonomous. The lady's feelings may be banal, but she is at least able to connect them to adequate objective correlatives, and so to achieve a kind of integration denied to the poet:

'*Yet with these April sunsets, that somehow recall*
My buried life, and Paris in the Spring,
I feel immeasurably at peace, and find the world
To be wonderful and youthful, after all.'

To 'sit here, serving tea to friends' is a vacuous sort of function, but it is at least a function, and so enviable to a poet who will be left

sitting pen in hand
With the smoke coming down above the housetops;
Doubtful, for a while
Not knowing what to feel or if I understand
Or whether wise or foolish, tardy or too soon. . . .

In the poet's case, the rift between object and feeling remains disabling: in what precise way, for instance, does the image of the smoke over the housetops engage with his disturbed consciousness? Like the shirt-sleeved men of *Prufrock* it hovers between dumb objectivity and an obscure resonance of emotional meaning. Nevertheless, the issue of who has the advantage is not decided: satiric criticism is switched to the poet, but the satire previously directed at the lady is not thereby cancelled. The speaker has been constrained to respect the autonomy of a social world beyond himself, and his malicious imagery, forcing that world into the mould of his own consciousness, is criticised; yet given this chastened sense of the lady's independent life, there is still no object there with which his feelings can significantly engage. What he engages with is not the emotions of the lady ('They all were sure our feelings would relate/So closely!') but with his own estrangement: the poem's objective correlative, once more, is the condition of being without one. Like Prufrock, the poet is both too far and too little distanced from the experience to evaluate it adequately: too far distanced, in that all he encounters in the relationship is a blankness; too little distanced, in that he has seen the falsity of believing that he is securely outside the described scene, as a satirically dissecting observer. He is forced to admit his involvement, even if it is only the involvement of non-response; he is drawn, unwillingly, into the event, made to see, as the reader is, the common ground between his own emotional reticence and the lady's emotional exhibitionism. Both, finally, are symptoms of a common collapse of communication and identity. In this sense, the two modes of satire—of the Society lady and of the narrator—cancel each other out, as they threaten to do in *Prufrock*. The lady, as the title of the poem and its literary allusion suggests, assumes a kind of pathetic dignity in contrast to the poet's hard-boiled obliquities of feeling, but the poet's right to smile is not wholly undermined: the lady remains a symbol of emotional banality, and so justifies in part the poet's defensively self-concealing tactics. In so far as she, too, manipulates feeling and creates falsely selective images of others, the speaker's attitude is endorsed.

In both *Prufrock* and *Portrait of a Lady*, Eliot explores the problem of the objective correlative through the use of a persona. Both poems present characters who are both too intimate with and estranged from their situations to formulate a judgement on it which is other than ironically ambiguous; both poems place this ambiguity in the context of establishing a satisfactory relation between object and feeling. In *Preludes*, however, Eliot abandons the persona and speaks directly— although 'directly' is, as we shall see, a slightly misleading term. The whole effort of *Preludes*, as I read the poem, is to achieve an objective correlative—particularised, local, sensory—of an insistent emotional state which has, at its extreme, the pressure of a 'vision'; but what is remarkable about the poem as a whole is its striking obliquity of approach. The first prelude sets a general scene:

> The winter evening settles down
> With smell of steaks in passageways.
> Six o'clock.
> The burnt-out ends of smoky days.
> And now a gusty shower wraps
> The grimy scraps
> Of withered leaves about your feet
> And newspapers from vacant lots;
> The showers beat
> On broken blinds and chimney-pots,
> And at the corner of the street
> A lonely cab-horse steams and stamps.
> And then the lighting of the lamps.

The overriding emphasis here is upon 'objectivity'; a tabulation of random but scrupulously placed details which together compose the diagram of an inert, depersonalised world. The interesting point (it is the point I shall fasten on in the poem as a whole) is the tension between this objectivity and a symbolic undertow which would transform it into a poetically significant *correlative*. In this first prelude, that undertow is on the whole resisted, detectable only in muted hints: 'withered leaves' and 'vacant lots' are almost too explicitly symbolic of a general human condition, but nothing is made of them; and the symbolic resonance of the lonely cab-horse is quickly dispersed by the mechanically neutral quality of the following line, whose 'And' suggests an unruffled, automatic, blandly natural process. When the verse advances more ambitiously general meanings, they are instantly counterpoised by sordid, stubbornly particular fragments: 'smell of steaks' quietly qualifies the wider gesture of 'winter evening', 'grimy scraps' tempers the metaphorical intensity of 'The burnt-out ends of smoky days'. The whole of this prelude, in other words, is concerned to

resist its own too easy conversion into an objective correlative
—a status which is intimated throughout, but never openly
confessed. It achieves a totalised statement of a kind, but only
in mood: otherwise, its details remain laconically disparate.

The second prelude effects a shift of level:

> *The morning comes to consciousness*
> *Of faint stale smells of beer*
> *From the sawdust-trampled street*
> *With all its muddy feet that press*
> *To early coffee-stands.*
> *With the other masquerades*
> *That time resumes,*
> *One thinks of all the hands*
> *That are raising dingy shades*
> *In a thousand furnished rooms.*

In the opening two lines, the first prelude's device of blending
abstraction and concretion, generalised image and sordid particular, is repeated, and a continuity thus established. What
'comes to consciousness', significantly, is not 'I' or 'he' but 'the
morning': an impersonalised collective image, derived from
'the evening' of *Prufrock*. Consciousness cannot yet be per-
sonalised, for this would be to derange the cautious objectivity
of the poem's texture; but with the introduction of the fact of
consciousness, we have moved slightly from the objectivations
of the first prelude towards, but not yet into, the realm of the
subjective. In the same way, personal agency is not, as yet,
allowed fully to enter the poem: human beings are glimpsed
only in the half-humanised actions of feet and hands, which
press and raise with the distanced automatism of the first section's beating rain and driving wind. It is this ambiguity which
registers itself in the last five lines, hovering as they do on the
brink of a subjective attitude without breaking too abruptly
with the composed neutrality of what has preceded them.
'Masquerades' is the first explicitly evaluative word in the
poem, and the final image underscores its sense of ritual futility;
but it manages to do so by making what is formally still a

neutrally descriptive statement, prefaced by an impersonal
'One thinks'. (In the shift from the 'your' of the first prelude
—a mere device to attach an event to some conveniently indeterminate body—to the 'One' of this section, a tentative
emergence into personal consciousness is again reflected.)

The second section, then, edges to the brink of a subjective
attitude but stops there, preserving impersonality; the third prelude then moves directly into the issues of vision and correlative:

> *You tossed a blanket from the bed*
> *You lay upon your back, and waited;*
> *You dozed, and watched the night revealing*
> *The thousand sordid images*
> *Of which your soul was constituted;*
> *They flickered against the ceiling.*
> *And when all the world came back*
> *And the light crept up between the shutters*
> *And you heard the sparrows in the gutters,*
> *You had such a vision of the street*
> *As the street hardly understands;*
> *Sitting along the bed's edge, where*
> *You curled the papers from your hair,*
> *Or clasped the yellow soles of feet*
> *In the palms of both soiled hands.*

The pronoun still distances ('You' gets a quickening dramatic
sense without losing impersonality), and it is still 'the night'
which reveals; but within this qualifying context 'a vision of
the street' is now possible: the foregoing description becomes
at last a correlative. Yet it is not, clearly, a vision to be trusted:
the experience is at once insistent and ironically qualified. A
perception which coheres and surpasses routine understanding
is now possible ('You had such a vision of the street / As the
street hardly understands'), but its subjectivism ('The thousand
sordid images / Of which your soul was constituted') is stressed
to the point where what emerges is a disjunction, rather than
a marriage, of external and internal reality. The dingy room
and sordid imagery question the validity of the vision, which

is in any case still essentially inarticulate, and the final shabby particular has the prudently deflating role of previous material details. The world is drably valueless, but so, perhaps, is the inflated 'insight' to which it gives rise; like Prufrock's sense of the insistently significant, its urgency seems in direct proportion to its unreality.

In the final prelude, the private vision merges with the observed city:

> *His soul stretched tight across the skies*
> *That fade behind a city block,*
> *Or trampled by insistent feet*
> *At four and five and six o'clock;*
> *And short square fingers stuffing pipes,*
> *And evening newspapers, and eyes*
> *Assured of certain certainties,*
> *The conscience of a blackened street*
> *Impatient to assume the world.*
>
> *I am moved by fancies that are curled*
> *Around these images, and cling,*
> *The notion of some infinitely gentle,*
> *Infinitely suffering thing.*
>
> *Wipe your hands across your mouth, and laugh;*
> *The worlds revolve like ancient women*
> *Gathering fuel in distant lots.*

In these first two lines, soul and city, emotional condition and material world, are brought together: but the relation between them is still obscure. In one sense, the city has now become the public projection of a private view; but in another sense, nothing of its mechanical objectivity has thereby been altered. The feet, fingers and eyes still tramp, stuff and stare with the assured precision of computers, and the mysteriousness which might connect them to the vagaries of private feeling is really only the mystery of their meaningless self-sufficiency, which, like the empty composure of the lady's tea-serving function in *Portrait of a Lady*, both fascinates and repels. In a single moment of personal self-exposure, the poet then declares his sense of an objective correlative: 'I am moved by fancies that are curled / Around these images, and cling'. But it is not only that the relation between fancy and image remains intangibly elusive ('*some* infinitely gentle . . . thing'); it is also that he is moved, not by fancies which are *elicited* from these images, but which are projected on to them. This, indeed, is at the core of Eliot's whole theory of the objective correlative: in so far as it suggests a projection of private feeling into material formula, rather than a revelation of meanings in some way intrinsic to reality, it can never escape an undermining sense of its own arbitrariness. For this reason, the connection which cannot quite be forged in this particular image points to a problem of connection inherent in the theory itself. Because Eliot sees the real world as a complex of material codes which can carry sub-jective emotion, a sense of the inevitable externality of emotion to code—the lack of an inward and necessary link between feeling and object—can never quite be avoided. And this will be important in our later discussion of Eliot's handling of myth. So the moment of connection is unsuccessful: a totalised vision lapses into the pluralist fragmentation of 'worlds'. The poem withdraws, with an uncertain bravado ('Wipe your hand across your mouth, and laugh') from first-person to second-person pronoun, and from the crisis of almost-articulate state-ment to a wry reassertion of the enduring neutrality of exist-ence, its resistance to the poet's designs on it.

Rhapsody on a Windy Night is another poem which seems best interpreted in terms of the problem of establishing the objective correlative. It is significant, to begin with, that what correlatives the poem succeeds in positing can emerge only through a radical dislocation of the material world: through an artificial 'lunar synthesis', disordering time, reason and meaning, in which reality is withdrawn and dissolved:

> *Twelve o'clock.*
> *Along the reaches of the street*
> *Held in a lunar synthesis,*

> *Whispering lunar incantations*
> *Dissolve the floors of memory*
> *And all its clear relations,*
> *Its divisions and precisions,*
> *Every street lamp that I pass*
> *Beats like a fatalistic drum,*
> *And through the spaces of the dark*
> *Midnight shakes the memory*
> *As a madman shakes a dead geranium.*

Even then, the connections which can be forged are mechanical rather than 'chemical':

> *. . . The street-lamp said, 'Regard that woman*
> *Who hesitates towards you in the light of the door*
> *Which opens on her like a grin.*
> *You see the border of her dress*
> *Is torn and stained with sand,*
> *And you see the corner of her eye*
> *Twists like a crooked pin.'*

The resource here is to the single-point relations of simile, not to organic fusion: sense-impressions remain stubbornly discrete:

> *The reminiscence comes*
> *Of sunless dry geraniums*
> *And dust in crevices,*
> *Smells of chestnuts in the streets,*
> *And female smells in shuttered rooms. . . .*

The 'lunar synthesis', then, generates the deceptive unity of moonshine, as the qualifying emphasis of the poem's title, *Rhapsody*, implies; 'synthetic' must be grasped simultaneously in both its senses, as the connection of elements into an integrated whole and as an *artificial* compounding. The whispering incantations are as insidiously misleading as the muttering streets of *Prufrock* or history's 'contrived corridors' and 'whispering ambitions' in *Gerontion*. Time is not, in fact, suspended, but lurches mechanically forward throughout the poem, the structure within which the pointless mergings take place, neither subdued by, nor subduing them, to intelligible order. The drunken walk home culminates in the final irony of sleep:

> *You have the key,*
> *The little lamp spreads a ring on the stair.*
> *Mount.*
> *The bed is open; the tooth-brush hangs on the wall,*
> *Put your shoes at the door, sleep, prepare for life.'*
> *The last twist of the knife.*

The poem has exploited the banal imagery of real life for a potentially valuable poetry of the unconscious, but the true rhythm of existence is the reverse: the unconsciousness of sleep as preparation for a worthless reality.

III

In his poems of 1920, Eliot seems to have moved closer to an achieved impersonality and to a more assured use of the object-ive correlative. *Gerontion* articulates an emptiness which belongs in part to the Prufrock world, but now with magnificently authoritative control. Gerontion himself is at one point merely symptomatic of the disintegration he records—'a dull head among windy spaces'—but unlike Prufrock he can also speak out of, and in part totalise, that collapse, as a truly representa-tive voice. He is part of the experience he expresses, and that is his title to speak; but he can also surmount it, through the superb confidences of image and metre, to the point where, in the middle passage on history, his own broken voice can blend (without unjustified appropriation) with the controlling and evaluating voice of the poet himself. In *Gerontion*, Eliot discovers that point of balance, between a helpless involvement with breakdown and a lofty estrangement in its face, which was not on the whole available in the earlier poetry. Neither Gerontion's nor the poet's voice is allowed to predominate: the issue is not simply 'placed' by a patrician externality, for these are still 'thoughts of a dry brain', and the energy is one of restlessly allusive suggestion, not of definition; but neither does Gerontion's own spiritual exhaustion prevent an impressively generalising gesture outwards, linking his own condition to a common historical loss. If that loss cannot ultimately be accounted for within the poem, it can at least be rendered into the fragmentary precisions of a poetry at once personal and impersonal, lyrical and reflective.

I have discussed some of Eliot's early poetry, up to *The Waste Land*, in terms of a search for the objective correlative: a search which involves the struggle for a poetic mode which will cohere object and emotion into an impersonal and 'objective' totality, establishing both distance and relation between the poet and his subject-matter. It is at this point, immediately before the writing of *The Waste Land*, that the relevance of this exploration to the discovery of myth can best be considered. For myth seems to provide the framework for precisely that kind of objective, impersonal and integrated poetic organisation, constructed from symbolic units which are themselves objective correlatives: figures and events around which common feelings have crystallised, and through which they can be instantly evoked. To this extent, myth is itself an entire objective correlative: a set of interwoven codes, expressive of emotional meanings, in which ordinary experience can be shaped into a coherent whole.

Jessie Weston's *From Ritual to Romance* appeared in 1920, just when Eliot was seeking a coordinating principle to unite the material of *The Waste Land*; and that he found such a principle in Weston's discussion of fertility cults and the Grail legend, combined with Frazer's study of vegetation rites, is, of course, well known. By drawing on the resources of myth, Eliot was able to totalise experience which remained otherwise disparate and unruly, welding it into an articulated structure: and this, indeed, is what *The Waste Land* shows. But this use of myth as a unifying principle is surely highly questionable. To begin with, what unity it creates from its subject-matter is really imposed from the outside: the coherence emerges, not from any genuine exploration of the inner structure of Western culture itself—from an attempt to find and render its internal coherence and intelligibility—but from the working through of that experience in terms of an external and predetermined pattern. The connections, insights, meanings of Western culture itself are thus subdued to the mythic framework: those relations and meanings most amenable to it—the imagery of sexual sterility, for example—are stressed, others less amenable are silently excluded.

The objection that Eliot's use of myth as a totalising pattern is imposed and therefore distorting can meet with the response that the myths he uses, far from being foisted on to his material, lie at the heart of all human society. This, indeed, is a fundamental principle behind some of the anthropology which interested Eliot, and it is an important element in the general argument. For to deny the tendentiousness implicit in this procedure, by asserting the universality of the mythic content, is really only to reveal another kind of tendentiousness: the belief that men, always and everywhere, are basically alike. This, indeed, is part of the rationale for employing a body of myth drawn from one epoch and culture to interpret another: and it is a position which Eliot certainly held. He believed in a 'common principle underlying all manifestations of life' (to quote Jessie Weston's own phrase), a principle which the uniformities supposedly revealed by anthropology could be seen to confirm. And it was that substratum of common consciousness, underlying the relatively insignificant variations of particular cultures, which he saw the artist as expressing. In a review of Wyndham Lewis, published in *The Egoist* in 1918, Eliot wrote: 'The artist, I believe, is *more* primitive, as well as more civilised, than his contemporaries; his experience is deeper than civilisation, and he only uses the phenomena of civilisation in expressing it'. Elsewhere, in his social and theoretical writing, Eliot persistently emphasises unity and similarity at the expense of what he sees as the Romantic error of individual uniqueness and variety; when a participant in the *Dialogue on Dramatic Poetry* maintains that human feeling has altered little from Aeschylus to the present day, it is, clearly enough, the author who speaks.

It is evident enough that this belief of Eliot's, which the supposedly neutral evidence of particular anthropological schools is taken as verifying, is deeply related to his general conservatism. To believe that men are always and everywhere much the same is to believe that radical change (with the exception of spiritual, extracultural change) is an illusion; it is also to undermine the significance of particular cultures and histories in the light of a primitive, permanent and universal substratum of consciousness. That consciousness can be easily translated into the social imagery of a traditional conservative wisdom; and in Eliot's later thought it has important relations to his religious faith. For this brand of mythical thinking, specific life-forms are merely surface variants (one might also say, when the position is at its hardest, 'deviants') of a deeper, persisting structure into which they root—a structure which finds symbolic incarnation in myth itself. That this attitude to particular forms of life should be held by a poet, whose business is supposedly with such specificities, seems itself ominous; but this is not precisely the main point to be made here. The main point is that, by this particular handling of myth, Eliot in *The Waste Land* is able to project a whole range of deeply subjective attitudes under the cover of a kind of neutrality. The 'neutrality' lies in the unspoken assumption that the mythic structures in question are universal, and so free from the relativism and partiality of local cultural judgements: they embody not just particular truths but fundamental structures of human life, always and everywhere applicable. The poet, on this view, speaks not from a position of vested interest within a culture, nor even from a definable cultural standpoint outside it, but from the primitive matrix of all human existence; and to this extent what he says seems unassailable. But this apparent disinterestedness rests, as I have suggested, on a highly specific and controversial view of man: it projects a conservative version of human culture in the guise of neutral fact.

The objection to Eliot's use of myth in *The Waste Land*, then, is not only that it is in some important respects external but that it smuggles private attitudes into what postures as impartial wisdom. Since the myth furnishes some of the structural elements of the poem (Eliot talks of it as providing his 'plan'), it inevitably communicates attitudes which the content itself may be less ready to express: the belief, for instance, that the cultural decline at issue is primarily 'spiritual' in source, that man has become artificially dislocated from the seasonal cycle, that history re-enacts itself in a futile way, that Margate and Carthage can be relevantly paralleled and contrasted, that a primary need is for an ascetic spiritual wisdom, that aspects of oriental culture have therefore something significant to offer. All these, and other attitudes are, of course, open to question: but they are embedded in the *structure* of the poem in a way which makes it more difficult to identify their assumptions than if they were directly communicated.

The assumption of *The Waste Land* is that no principle of coherence can be found within Western culture itself: all classes of society, from debutantes and businessmen to clerks and working-people, are passively implicated in the same deep-rooted corruption. This is an attitude carried and expressed, not only in what is explicitly said, but in the 'totalising' framework which allows for such a detached and omniscient view of an entire culture. Yet while the attitude is the result of what this framework allows the poet to see, it is also the inevitable result: if you stand this far back, nothing will seem particularly valuable. The mythic structure can connect itself significantly with social experience only by first paring that experience to its own requirements:

> I, Tiresias, old man with wrinkled dugs
> Perceived the scene, and foretold the rest—
> I too awaited the expected guest.
> He, the young man carbuncular, arrives,
> A small house agent's clerk, with one bold stare,
> One of the low on whom assurance sits

As a silk hat on a Bradford millionaire.
The time is now propitious, as he guesses,
The meal is ended, she is bored and tired,
Endeavours to engage her in caresses
Which still are unreproved, if undesired.
Flushed and decided, he assaults at once;
Exploring hands encounter no defence;
His vanity requires no response,
And makes a welcome of indifference.
(And I Tiresias have foresuffered all
Enacted on this same divan or bed;
I who have sat by Thebes below the wall
And walked among the lowest of the dead.)

The foresufferance of Tiresias in no sense 'places' the observed experience: the dull rhythms of his casually bracketed comment follow inexorably, without a shift of tone, from what precedes them, and the comment itself merely asserts an omniscience which, in terms of what is actually said, has no point of critical purchase on the scene. It is the irrelevance of his remark which is most striking: a formal relation of the incident to 'history' which makes no substantial connection at all. But it is, precisely, in that formal and empty relation that the 'significance' of the passage, and of Tiresias's presence, is supposed to emerge: once more, 'meaning' is carried primarily in a device of structure rather than in explicit content. Tiresias, like the figures of some of Eliot's early poetry, is both too intimate with and too estranged from what he observes to offer a constructive criticism. He is part of its listless rhythm, and that rhythm is a vibration of his own consciousness; but at the same time he is so wholly involved, as the zone of perception in which the incident takes place, that he has no effective presence *within* the incident, and so, paradoxically, is banished as an impotent observer to its periphery. He stands in the same relation to the event as a man might stand in relation to the alien images of his own mind: too close to intervene among them as a separate agent, yet precisely because of that over-closeness, passively divorced from control and comprehension. Like the 'familiar compound ghost' of *Little Gidding*, the event is both 'intimate and unidentifiable': both a projection, and an alienation, of the poet's feeling. The effect of this ambivalence is that what is really a profoundly estranged version of human activity can be offered as a suffering solidarity with it. Tiresias's refusal explicitly to judge and 'place' the behaviour of the clerk and typist emerges as a wearily all-encompassing wisdom, and even grants the couple a kind of historic significance, through its classical reference; but that refusal to judge is in fact merely an aspect of the more fundamental detachment which creates the incident in the first place. The whole event is, in an exact sense, myth: the manipulation of social experience into a system of predetermined symbolic categories whose interrelations 'explain' its significance. 'Carbuncular', 'small house agent's clerk', 'silk hat', 'low', 'Bradford millionaire': these are stock units drawn from a conventional social typology, each with its fixed and single signification; they have then only to be permutated and combined, according to the rules of the mythology, for the 'meaning' to appear. The objection which can be registered to this is then the criticism which can be made of much of the poem: in so far as the limits of the mythology remain unquestioned, the whole projection (as its automatic rhythms tend to imply) is 'natural', and Tiresias's detachment the impotence of an observer of how life 'really' is; in so far as that social mythology is questioned, his detachment becomes, not a quality of response, but a quality of the tendentious mind out of which the incident is created.

The Waste Land, then, mediates the experience of personal and cultural collapse through the terms of a body of myth at once social and anthropological: and what is most interesting is the interaction between these two typologies. The typology drawn from Weston and Frazer is essentially static: it grasps the realities of disintegration, not historically, as a process to be examined and understood on its own terms, but mythically, in terms of energies and conditions which are only incidentally

cultural. When an historical connection is suggested—between
Thebes and London, Carthage and Margate—it is of no more
than 'symbolic' importance: the facility with which it can be
asserted is itself an index of the absence of any genuinely historical consciousness at work. This anthropological framework
of myth, with its reservations about the value of history and
change, its pattern of fixed and permanent types, then engages
with the poem's socially conservative ideology, with its equally
fixed and limited range of figures: the caricatured working-
women of *A Game of Chess*, the seedy, sexually licentious
foreigner Mr Eugenides, the neurotic Society dame, the shabby
typist. Between them they constitute a stalely unintelligent,
contemptuously patronising version of contemporary society:
a neat, Arnoldian totality (Barbarians, Philistines, Populace)
which is really no more than an ensemble of stock Shavian
portraits. Yet because they are all, in one way or another,
associated with primitive or classical myth—the typist with
Thebes, the Society woman with Philomel, Mr Eugenides with
the currants of a vegetation ceremony, the working-women
with the natural cycles of birth, copulation and death—they
gain a spurious deepening of significance which seems to excuse
the one-dimensional quality of their presentation. The controlling mythology, in other words, refines the density of real social
experience to the outline of its own archetypes, and we are
expected to acquiesce in the process; but whether we acquiesce
or not, the truth seems to be that the thin texture of social
reality with which we are left is all that Eliot is in any case
capable of imagining. And in this sense, 'myth' excuses a
genuine superficiality. The social and anthropological myths
are mutually validating: the thinness of the first seems justified
by its function in reflecting the second; and conversely, because
'society' is arranged so precisely to fit the facts of 'myth', it
appears inevitably to verify it.

    The mythology of Eliot's next major poem, *Ash Wednesday*,
is drawn from the Christian Church rather than from *The Golden
Bough*, but there is a sense in which part of what has been said

of *The Waste Land* applies here too. In a perceptive discussion of the poem in his *Poetry and the Sacred*, Vincent Buckley talks of its 'unmistakable tendency to resort to scriptural and liturgical terms whenever the stress of emotion becomes too acute', and of its occasional 'wordy circlings round an undefined crisis, the pretentious conversion of Christian tradition into a private mythology'.[1] Mr Buckley's description seems to me in the main accurate: and it relates to what has been said already of Eliot's early search for the objective correlative, and of his use of myth in *The Waste Land*. In the earlier poetry, as I have argued, the problem of the relation between private feeling and an 'objective' structure of imagery becomes itself, often enough, the substance of a poem: the search for a method by which subjective emotion might objectify itself in an impersonal and integrating formula failed, and it failed in part because social reality seemed too inert, or too fragmented, to permit of such a totalisation. In *The Waste Land*, I have suggested, the problem of the relation between private attitude and generalising public code is solved by the use of myth, but solved in ways which leave the impersonal objectivity of the symbolic codes open to question. In *Ash Wednesday*, as Mr Buckley implies, the relation is again inadequately defined. It is not exactly that in this poem Eliot arbitrarily projects certain personal assumptions through a supposedly universal structure; for the point of the liturgical and doctrinal imagery of the Christian poem is that it is at once communally shared and yet permeated with personal devotional feeling. It is rather that, in *Ash Wednesday*, a refining of the density of actual experience to fit it to a mythic pattern is carried at times even further than in *The Waste Land*. It is carried, in fact, to the point where the manipulation of symbolic formulas seems occasionally to have wholly subsituted itself for the experience:

> *Will the veiled sister between the slender*
> *Yew trees pray for those who offend her*

[1] London, 1968, pp. 213-19.

And are terrified and cannot surrender
And affirm before the world and deny between the rocks
In the last desert between the last blue rocks
The desert in the garden the garden in the desert
Of drouth, spitting from the mouth the withered apple-seed.

The imagery here seems self-generating: 'yew', 'rocks', 'desert', 'garden' and 'apple-seed', like the silk hat and Bradford million- aire of *The Waste Land*, are fixed, flat units of signification, and the poetic energy goes wholly into the empty dexterity with which they are permutated. It is a quality common in the poem:

Who walked between the violet and the violet
Who walked between
The various ranks of varied green
Going in white and blue, in Mary's colour,
Talking of trivial things
In ignorance and in knowledge of eternal dolour
Who moved among the others as they walked,
Who then made strong the fountains and made fresh the springs

'Then', in that final line, comes as a surprise: it suggests, abruptly, that the rarefied ritual of the previous lines was a process of actual events. The whole passage has a purely ab- stract, emblematical quality which makes it characteristic of some of the worst flaws of *Ash Wednesday* as a whole: its elaborate mannerisms of internal rhyme, its displacements of emotional dialectic into a kind of superior intellectual punning, its ritualised verbosity. The objection, it should be stressed, is not to the emblematical mode as such: indeed, some of the poem's most deeply admirable effects spring precisely from that source:

At the first turning of the third stair
Was a slotted window bellied like the fig's fruit
And beyond the hawthorn blossom and a pasture scene
The broadbacked figure drest in blue and green
Enchanted the maytime with an antique flute.
Blown hair is sweet, brown hair over the mouth blown,

Lilac and brown hair;
Distraction, music of the flute, stops and steps of the mind over
the third stair,
Fading, fading; strength beyond hope and despair
Climbing the third stair.

The strength of this is in the way it offers its emblems in an unforced structure of natural interrelations, exploiting their simple vigour and mutual enrichment without manipulation. Its candidness suggests a very different quality from the cerebral involutions of desert, rocks and garden; and the essential difference is that here the emblematical mode is recognised for what it is, in both its strengths and limits. The poem fails most evidently where it tries to marshal its emblems into a complex activity of meaning which they cannot sustain—forces them, in fact, to behave as symbols. What we get then is the impression of essentially simple units of meaning being dragooned into disproportionately involved patterns, and a consequent sense of a combining and multiplying energy overwhelming its subject-matter:

Where shall the word be found, where will the word
Resound? Not here, there is not enough silence
Not on the sea or on the islands, not
On the mainland, in the desert or the rain land,
For those who walk in darkness
Both in the day time and in the night time
The right time and the right place are not here
No place of grace for those who avoid the face
No time to rejoice for those who walk among noise and deny
the voice

The richness lacking in individual images—'sea', 'desert', 'rain land', 'voice'—has to be compensated for by a factitious, almost frenetic interplay of word and sound.

Ash Wednesday, then, reveals a damaging imbalance of personal experience and mythological formula: the latter seems too often to substitute itself for the former, the pressures of thought and feeling to be taken too regularly by a range of objective correlatives inadequate to their demands. It is here, in fact, that the poem differs most from *Four Quartets*. Whereas *Ash Wednesday* seems to externalise its feeling too readily into a ritual and imagery which must then bear the whole weight of the experience, the role of imagery in the *Quartets* is to enact and illustrate meanings which are discursively, as well as symbolically, formulated. The function of image, in other words, is strictly limited: its purpose is to express, and interact with, a pattern of significance created by other means:

> *To be conscious is not to be in time*
> *But only in time can the moment in the rose-garden,*
> *The moment in the arbour where the rain beat,*
> *The moment in the draughty church at smokefall*
> *Be remembered; involved with past and future.*
> *Only through time time is conquered.*
>
> (*Burnt Norton*)

> *. . . there is a time for building*
> *And a time for living and for generation*
> *And a time for the wind to break the loosened pane*
> *And to shake the wainscot where the field-mouse trots*
> *And to shake the tattered arras woven with a silent motto.*
>
> (*East Coker*)

> *. . . Not the intense moment*
> *Isolated, with no before and after,*
> *But a lifetime burning in every moment*
> *And not the lifetime of one man only*
> *But of old stones that cannot be deciphered.*
>
> (*East Coker*)

> *The moment of the rose and the moment of the yew-tree*
> *Are of equal duration. A people without history*
> *Is not redeemed from time, for history is a pattern*
> *Of timeless moments. So, while the light fails*
> *On a winter's afternoon, in a secluded chapel*
> *History is now and England.*
>
> (*Little Gidding*)

The imagery of all these passages is quietly restrained, curtailed to the function of emblem and exemplar; the tension between concrete particular and generalising abstraction is in each case exact. The concrete image is not loaded with a complex pressure of meaning which it alone must carry: its significance works within the firm texture of poised reflection, as a notation, a vivid instance, a confirming gesture. Yet at the same time there is nothing arbitrary about the selection of these sudden crystallisations: there is no sense of that casually patrician carelessness with the actual, that oblique and fortuitous choice of material image, which disfigures some of Eliot's earlier writing. The imagery of *Four Quartets* does not operate with the condensed, cryptic power of the *symboliste* Eliot: at times, indeed, it has the simple abstract force of a kind of shorthand:

> *We cannot revive old factions*
> *We cannot restore old policies*
> *Or follow an antique drum.*
>
> (*Little Gidding*)

But while it remains at a level below the complex embodiments of that earlier symbolism, either candidly emblematic ('The moment of the rose and the moment of the yew–tree ...') or forcefully illustrative ('old stones that cannot be deciphered'), it has no merely external or gratuitous relation to its subject-matter. 'The moment in the arbour where the rain beat' is a choice of one image from a range of possibilities, and the quietly dramatic shift from abstract to concrete which accompanies it, with its hint of deliberate, slight disjunction, is meant to hold the fact of that limitation before our attention; we are not to think that this single image incarnates all of what is there. Yet equally, all these images achieve an inward and organic relation to the poem's reflections: they are neither random exemplars nor uniquely enacting modes.

The upshot of this is that, throughout *Four Quartets*, the objective correlative in its initial definition is effectively abandoned. It is no longer a question of discovering the unique material formulas which will express and encapsulate feeling: for that feeling is as much available outside particular symbols, in a discursive poetry of elegantly abstract enquiry. And one consequence of this is that feeling no longer shelters behind modes of ritual and myth which in earlier poems were either speciously objective projections of, or substitutions for, honest personal declaration. It is the honesty of *Four Quartets* —their blending of achieved statement with a vulnerable exposure of those tentative processes of feeling which went into the achievement—which is at once most striking and (to add the more controversial qualification), most un-Eliotic. If the achieved, totalised and impersonal statement recalls *The Waste Land*, the exposed and hesitant movements towards formulation recall the earlier poetry; and in the light of this poem, the one-sidedness of both of those earlier modes—the spurious impersonality of the one, the subjective fragmentations of the other—can be clearly seen. *Four Quartets* has its obvious flaws: there is a sense in which the sonorous latinisms of this passage, for instance, recall the verbose evasions of *Ash Wednesday*:

> *Descend lower, descend only*
> *Into the world of perpetual solitude,*
> *World not world, but that which is not world,*
> *Internal darkness, deprivation*
> *And destitution of all property,*
> *Desiccation of the world of sense,*
> *Evacuation of the world of fancy,*
> *Inoperancy of the world of spirit. . . .*
>
> (*Burnt Norton*)

Here, once more, a verbal ritual substitutes itself for genuine response; and it is significant that the passage completes a section which in the first three poems is given over to a kind of social satire with all the remote and sterile banality of some of Eliot's earlier poetry. On the other hand, the evasions of this verbal or mythical patterning, this too-eager grasping at a neatly totalised meaning—

Scorpion fights against the Sun
Until the Sun and Moon go down
Comets weep and Leonids fly
Hunt the heavens and the plains
Whirled in a vortex that shall bring
The world to that destructive fire
Which burns before the ice-cap reigns

(East Coker)

—is now seen for what it is: 'A periphrastic study in a worn-out poetical fashion, / Leaving one still with the intolerable wrestle / With words and meanings'.

The tensions between concrete and abstract meanings in *Four Quartets*, between a focused moment and its sustaining context, has an evident relation to a problem at the core of the poem: the relation between an existential present and the sense of a totalised historical pattern. It is impossible to examine that theme in any detail here; but it is worth pointing its relevance to what we have said of Eliot's earlier poetry. For this, in a sense, was always Eliot's problem: the difficulty of enforcing genuine connections between fragments of 'subjective' or 'objective' reality (the broken feelings of *Prufrock* or the inert material atoms of *Preludes*) and a total structure of meaning. I have argued that some of these early poems concern a failure to transcend their own fragments, and that both *The Waste Land* and *Ash Wednesday* do so only by using a mythic framework which can damage the autonomy of those fragments by projecting an extrinsic pattern upon them. By the time of *Four Quartets*, however, the whole issue has significantly altered. In a late statement of his views on 'pattern' in experience, Eliot speaks of the function of art as 'imposing a credible order upon ordinary reality, and thereby eliciting some perception of an order *in* reality' (*On Poetry and Poets*). The first half of this statement has its source in the concerns of Eliot's pre-religious period; the second springs from his conversion to the Christian faith. Eliot's 'order *in* reality' is not, of course, primarily the order created and received by the historical actions of men, but a transcendental immanence; yet given this view, it is interesting that he now sees the method of establishing significant order in reality as dialectical. The poet's task is neither merely to impose nor passively to reveal a pattern: genuine revelation emerges through acts of creative consciousness, which are in turn guarded against the charge of subjectivism by the confirming reality of a 'given' structure within history itself. It is to this, changed view of the nature of totalisation that the achievement of *Four Quartets* is in part indebted. In that poem, 'the pattern is new in every moment', for each existential present re-casts and re-totalises its contours; yet history is still, nevertheless, 'a *pattern* of timeless moments', not an unstructured congeries of them. The technical problem, of relating a particular image or emblem to the pattern of a general argument, enacts this tension. The autonomy of each, illustrative image must be preserved, but also tactfully subdued to a function within the wider movement of revelation; the particular image must neither merely 'exemplify', nor arrogantly substitute itself for, the complete experience. In this way, that balance which was sought through the objective correlative—the structure of feeling neither twisting the object to its own shape, nor the object dominating or concealing the structure of feeling—can be exactly achieved. It is a balance which *Little Gidding* is able to articulate, with the authority of its own genius behind it, in a reflection on the medium in which, for the poet, all these issues begin and end—language itself:

> . . . *And every phrase*
> *And sentence that is right (where every word is at home,*
> *Taking its place to support the others,*
> *The word neither diffident nor ostentatious,*
> *An easy commerce of the old and the new,*
> *The common word exact without vulgarity,*
> *The formal word precise but not pedantic,*
> *The complete consort dancing together)*
> *Every phrase and every sentence is an end and a beginning,*
> *Every poem an epitaph.*

IV

Eliot's use of myth is one major example of a constant exploitation of this source in the twentieth century, of which the two other principal exponents are Joyce and Yeats. Yet important distinctions, relevant to the critical questions we have raised, need to be made between the uses of myth in each of these writers' work.

In a note on *Ulysses*, Eliot admired its deployment of myth as a way of lending cohesion to the 'vast panorama of anarchy and futility that is contemporary civilisation'. What he appreciated in the novel, in other words, was primarily the parallel it offered to his own *Waste Land* technique. That such a parallelism exists is unquestionable: the purposes to which myth is put in *Ulysses*—to cohere, to universalise, to generate both contrast and comparison between past and present—have an obvious similarity to Eliot's. Yet there is a paradoxical sense in which Joyce is most different from Eliot where he seems most alike: in the flagrantly imposed quality of the mythic structure itself. The outrageousness of *Ulysses* is that the myth by which the experience of Dublin is welded into synthetic unity has no inward and necessary conjunction with that experience at all: one could imagine Joyce having put a quite different myth to the same purpose, with the same exhaustive ingenuity. And this, indeed, is part of the novel's point: the relation between myth and experience is so patently gratuitous that their interpenetration can only be asethetically, rather than 'realistically', convincing. It is possible, of course, to raise critical questions about the flamboyant artifice of that literary method; but it is hardly possible to doubt that it *is*, self-consciously, artificial, in a way that Eliot's does not at points *appear* to be. Joyce's use of myth is so purely synthetic that it can hardly be mistaken for a hermeneutic principle which elicits a structure of meanings intrinsic to Dublin itself; it is so openly imposed on the subject-matter that the overall disjunction is comically evident.

It is, explicitly, a *tour de force*, a triumph of aesthetic manipulation. In one sense, indeed, myth and experience are so minutely interwoven that the disjunction is not *locally* apparent: the myth is translated with such deft precision into the detail of Bloomsday that it is hard to find a specific point at which one can *feel* that detail being 'rigged'. But when the two dimensions, of myth and Dublin, are looked at as distinct wholes, the arbitrariness of connection is immediately evident.

The result of this self-conscious artifice of imposition is that Joyce, unlike Eliot, does not on the whole exploit the mythical device as a way of projecting private attitudes beneath a cover of impersonality. It is true that elements of the mythic structure do, in a general sense, correspond to elements of Joyce's own way of seeing: the theme of paternity, the sense of cyclic totality, of reality as an immense *gestalt* of interlocking processes, and so on. But the generality of these correspondences is important: they do not usually emerge, as they do, say, in the typist-passage of *The Waste Land*, in a rigging of local detail to confirm a tendentious private view which is then offered as neutral— as a product of the European mind. On the contrary, what is striking about *Ulysses*—what is, in fact, part of its overall irony— is that its level of naturalistic reality, rigidly controlled as it is, in every quarter, by the exigencies of myth, remains densely and specifically autonomous. The myth is, as it were, so intimately moulded to Dublin life, so persistently and pervasively present, that to all intents and purposes it disappears. It is so intricately in command of the whole creation that its presence is at no particular point obtrusive. The contrast with Eliot is thus significant: for Eliot's use of myth to communicate a personal attitude can be felt, on occasions, in precisely that kind of unwarranted local intervention.

The uses of myth in *Finnegans Wake*, different as they are from *Ulysses*, are nevertheless more akin to that novel than to Eliot. *Finnegans Wake* seems to me best understood in the light of those modes of explaining and analysing myth developed by the structuralist school of anthropology.[1] What is operative in the novel is a kind of poetic rationality akin to what Lévi-Strauss has named *bricolage*: a ceaseless combination and permutation of the fragments of a multiple number of myths into a kind of meta-myth, a total structure with a number of interpenetrating levels, any one of which can be 'read off' in terms of any number of others. The whole novel stacks myths behind myths behind myths, combining, dissolving and integrating them in a number of simultaneous perspectives, such that an examination of the dialectical logic at work throughout the book would strictly require the sort of three-dimensional model which structural anthropologists have in fact constructed to grasp the endlessly complex workings of primitive mythologies. Lévi-Strauss points out that there is at work, in these primitive mythologies, a kind of dialectics by which the fragments which compose a particular mythical totality can be simultaneously 'decoded' on a number of other models, so that the whole system is in constant interaction; there is, that is to say, a mechanism inherent in the system which allows meanings to be constantly transferred from one level or structure to another. In *Finnegans Wake*, that dialectic is present as auditory allusion: each unit of sound has a multiple set of implications which permit it to be endlessly combined with other, similarly allusive units, to form structures which can in turn be broken down and reconstituted into larger or subsidiary myths. The function of *bricolage* is served here, essentially, by the pun. In the same way, a character in *Finnegans Wake* can exist simultaneously on four or five levels of mythical meaning: characters, like words, behave as symbols through which different levels of myth can be reciprocally mediated to one another. As in *Ulysses*, the whole of this mythical structure may be said to project certain of Joyce's own attitudes: a particular view of history, and of the nature of historical change, can no doubt be distilled from its complexities. Yet once more, those

[1] Cf. especially Claude Lévi-Strauss, *Structural Anthropology*: New York and London, 1963, and *The Savage Mind*, London, 1966.

attitudes can hardly be seen as the sustaining motivation of the uses of myth in the novel: as in *Ulysses*, they are too generalised in quality to be significantly related to its detail.

If Joyce's use of myth can be contrasted in some respects with Eliot's, the same can be said of Yeats. Like Eliot, Yeats uses myth to communicate deeply held personal attitudes; like him, too, he discovers in myth the sources of an energy urgently needed to renew an impoverished present. Where the Irish poet differs crucially, however, is in a candid declaration of the tendentious basis of that use:

> *I declare this tower is my symbol; I declare*
> *This winding, gyring, spiring treadmill of a stair is my ances-*
> *tral stair;*
> *That Goldsmith and the Dean, Berkeley and Burke have*
> *travelled there.*
>
> > (Blood and the Moon)

A private mythology constructed from public history is set up, but set up in full view of the reader: and to this extent its quality of defiant subjectivism (implicitly related, in a later stanza, to the philosophical idealism of Berkeley), is not covert but declared, in a tone of public honesty which, it must be said, is foreign to *The Waste Land*. Yeats, like Eliot, weaves historical and mythological imagery into the texture of the present: but the interrelations which these areas set up within his poetry are almost always more complex than in Eliot's. In both poets, the characteristic relation between mythical or historical past and present culture is almost invariably one of a comparison unfavourable to the contemporary; but whereas in Eliot's poetry, the relation is most typically one of simple contrast: past splendour set against present squalor—

> *But at my back from time to time I hear*
> *The sound of horns and motors, which shall bring*
> *Sweeny to Mrs Porter in the spring*

—in Yeats there is continuity, as well as rupture, between past and present, myth and social experience. It is because there is continuity—because Irish myth and contemporary Ireland are held together within the fabric of a single cultural history—that they can be interrelated without the 'placing' externality of Eliot's insinuating literary reference. Because they both belong to a single history, the contrast in which they can be placed, angrily, arrogantly or nostalgically, can still come through as a *relationship*, rather than as blank dislocation:

> *We were the last romantics—chose for theme*
> *Traditional sanctity and loveliness;*
> *Whatever's written in what poets name*
> *The book of the people; whatever most can bless*
> *The mind of man or elevate a rhyme;*
> *But all is changed, that high horse riderless,*
> *Though mounted in that saddle Homer rode*
> *Where the swan drifts upon a darkening flood.*
>
> (*Coole Park and Ballylee, 1931*)

Past culture in both history ('Traditional sanctity') and myth ('the book of the people'); but the final contrast with present devastation, though poignant, is not abrupt. On the contrary, the elegant energy of the first five lines spills over into, and strangely dignifies, the closing images: contemporary society is anarchic and adrift, but that feeling is still formulated in the eloquent rhetoric of emblem and myth. There is enough continuity of perception, in other words, to justify the fact that 'name' is in the present tense. A parallel instance can be found in *Meditations in Time of Civil War*:

> *The cloud-pale unicorns, the eyes of aquamarine,*
> *The quivering half-closed eyelids, the rags of cloud or of lace,*
> *Or eyes that rage has brightened, arms it has made lean,*
> *Give place to an indifferent multitude, give place*
> *To brazen hawks. Nor self-delighting reverie,*
> *Nor hate of what's to come, nor pity for what's gone,*
> *Nothing but grip of claw, and the eye's complacency,*
> *The innumerable clanging wings that have put out the moon.*

Mythology has yielded to a complacent violence—yet that, also, is imaged in terms which effortlessly catch up the mythical style, enforcing continuity in the act of mourning its loss.

Myth, in Yeats, is not easily disengaged from history, and neither are easily separable from the present. It can be argued that a function of myth in general is to arrest and distance living history into permanent forms; but in a poem like *In Memory of Major Robert Gregory,* a ritual, mourning formality, gathering Gregory into the realm of mythology, can be achieved with no loss to the sense of his vivid historical presence. The whole poem becomes a structure within which legend, history and myth interact with an insistent and representative present loss, each element half-creating the others. Yeats's poetry can align history and myth against the present (Mrs French and Hanrahan in *The Tower,* Parnell and Troy in *Three Marching Songs*), but there are other possibilities, too:

> *I have met them at close of day*
> *Coming with vivid faces*
> *From counter or desk among grey*
> *Eighteenth-century houses.*
> *I have passed with a nod of the head*
> *Or polite meaningless words,*
> *Or have lingered awhile and said*
> *Polite meaningless words,*
> *And thought before I had done*
> *Of a mocking tale or a gibe*
> *To please a companion*
> *Around the fire at the club,*
> *Being certain that they and I*
> *But lived where motley is worn,*
> *All changed, changed utterly,*
> *A terrible beauty is born.*

> (*Easter 1916*)

It is, finally, this rare capacity to watch one's own derided present come alive as both history and myth—to see a common experience, lived with full involvement from the inside, in the transfiguring terms of an outsider's perspective—which distin-

guishes Yeats from Eliot. It is in Yeats's respect for and implication with the history of his culture, even at the crisis of rejection and despair, that he differs most from the poet of *The
Waste Land*. Eliot, indeed, constantly explored the nature of
that historical consciousness in his critical and theoretical work,
and an affirmation of it is to be found in almost the last poetic
statement he made: 'History is now and England'. But it is not,
on the whole, a predominant position in his poetry: it is a
position which he spent his poetic life striving to achieve. With
Yeats, myth serves the function of clarifying a relation between
history and the present; with Eliot, myth tends to usurp history
itself.

Eliot's use of myth, then, makes him a significant figure in
this study. In contrast to the writers whom we have previously
examined, Eliot was able to achieve a total statement of his
society: to explore and communicate what, at various stages
of his development in poetry and belief, he took to be its determining reality. His ability to do so rested in part upon his
stance as an expatriate: he came to European culture from a
viewpoint which, formed and nurtured as it undoubtedly was
by European intellectual and cultural history, was nevertheless
in certain central respects not of that milieu. That tension, I
have argued, has been one consistent formula for major literary
art in this century, and it was one which Eliot's work exploited.
But Eliot also demonstrates some of the ways in which that
tension could be imperfectly achieved: the way in which the
expatriate's vision could lead to estrangement and externality,
or the way in which he could share too deeply in the conservative, static assumptions of the culture he adopted to surmount
its rigidities of feeling. In this situation, Eliot was like his own
early poetic personae: too estranged from an inward understanding of English social life to make more than a caricatured
judgement on it, too intimate with some of its restrictive modes
of feeling to transcend them for a fuller vision. In his use of
myth, these two elements occasionally converged: an external,
cosmopolitan, even 'universal' seeing proper to the expatriate

became the carrier of attitudes close to the heart of a conservative society. In opposition to this, the emergent historical sense of *Little Gidding* defines a different Eliot: an Eliot with the breadth of perspective, the sharpened sense of both place and movement, settlement and horizon, of the genuine expatriate:

> *A people without history*
> *Is not redeemed from time, for history is a pattern*
> *Of timeless moments. So, while the light fails*
> *On a winter's afternoon, in a secluded chapel*
> *History is now and England.*

CHAPTER VI

A Note on Auden

About suffering they were never wrong,
The Old Masters: how well they understood
Its human position; how it takes place
While someone else is eating or opening a window or just
  walking dully along;
How, when the aged are reverently, passionately waiting
For the miraculous birth, there always must be
Children who did not specially want it to happen, skating
On a pond at the edge of the wood:
They never forgot
That even the dreadful martyrdom must run on its course
Anyhow in a corner, some untidy spot
Where the dogs go on with their doggy life and the torturer's
  horse
Scratches its innocent behind on a tree.

AUDEN lived through the suffering of an epoch, and was applauded, for many years, as its representative voice; yet the irony around which this first stanza of *Musée des Beaux Arts* revolves—the incongruous, uneven relationship between major human catastrophe and the casual detail of routine life—points to a difficulty in 'representativeness' central to much of his social poetry. The suffering is intensely real, and so is the 'untidy spot' which provides it with a context: yet the link between them can only be contingent and external, focusing maladjustment rather than connection. It is not difficult to trace the roots of this perception in the particular social condition out of which Auden wrote: the condition of a society undergoing a disturbance so profound that it required a real effort of attention and analysis to relate it at all significantly to the stubbornly persisting fabric of daily life. It is a version of George Bowling's problem, in *Coming Up For Air*: the problem of grasping, within a single frame of reference, the domestic facts of English society and the inconceivably total disaster with which it was confronted. But it is interesting that in *Musée des Beaux Arts* Auden sees the incongruity, not as especially symptomatic of such a social condition, but as an inevitable 'human position'; the point of the appeal to the Old Masters is to confirm this sense that the dislocation in question is of a universal and unchanging kind:

> In Brueghel's Icarus, for instance, how everything turns away
> Quite leisurely from the disaster; the ploughman may
> Have heard the splash, the forsaken cry
> But for him it was not an important failure; the sun shone
> As it had to on the white legs disappearing into the green
> Water; and the expensive delicate ship that must have
>   seen
> Something amazing, a boy falling out of the sky,
> Had somewhere to get to and sailed calmly on.

The most interesting equation here is between ploughman, ship and sun: the blank neutrality of Nature ('the sun shone / As it had to on the white legs . . .') is offered as an exact equivalent to human indifference. The total effect is then not to challenge this world of separated goals and involvements, but to ratify it, in a 'shrewdly' anti-heroic wisdom, as 'the way life is'.

It is not, of course, necessarily the way life is: if the particular suffering which Auden recorded seemed obstinately external to ordinary social life, it is equally true that there are other catastrophes, and other conflicts, which are both universal and specific, lived at once as a general condition and an immediate experience. One thinks, for instance, of the contrast between the war Auden knew, with its partial separation of domestic living and military campaign, and the Third World liberation struggles which have followed it, where no such distinction seems possible. But it was the way life seemed to Auden, living at that inevitable distance from the conflicts. Suffering, from

this viewpoint, appears either as private or intangibly pervasive:
a blunt, uninterpretable fact about individuals or an elusively
generalised mood. The first attitude is the stance of *Musée des
Beaux Arts*, but it finds other expressions in Auden's early work:

> They are and suffer; that is all they do;
> A bandage hides the place where each is living,
> His knowledge of the world restricted to
> The treatment that the instruments are giving.
>
> And lie apart like epochs from each other
> —Truth in their sense is how much they can bear;
> It is not talk like ours, but groans they smother—
> And are remote as plants; we stand elsewhere.
>
> For who when healthy can become a foot?
> Even a scratch we can't recall when cured,
> But are boist'rous in a moment and believe
> In the common world of the uninjured, and cannot
> Imagine isolation. Only happiness is shared,
> And anger, and the idea of love.
>
> *(Surgical Ward)*

The tough 'realist' tone invites assent, but the technique is
surely questionable. By a particular moral interpretation of the
physical posture of the wounded, the poem removes the facts
of physical suffering from any wider human context in which
they could be discussed and interpreted; and once this is done,
the externality of the healthy to the sick, the normal to the
terrible, follows logically enough. Sympathy, understanding
and connection, it is implied, are either irrelevant or sentimental; here, as in *Musée des Beaux Arts*, there can be no significant relation between the common world and catastrophe.

Auden's insistence here on the inviolable privacy of suffering,
his 'tough' rejection of efforts to comprehend it, goes with a
more tremulous sense, elsewhere in the poetry, of a disturbance
and suffering too deep and widespread for articulation:

> The journals give the quantities of wrong,
> Where the impatient massacre took place,

How many and what sort it caused to die,
But, O, what finite integers express
The realm of malice where these facts belong?
How can the mind make sense, bombarded by
A stream of incompatible mishaps,
The bloom and buzz of a confessed collapse?

What properties define our person since
This massive vagueness moved in on our lives,
What laws require our substance to exist?
Our strands of private order are dissolved
And lost our routes to self-inheritance,
Position and Relation are dismissed,
An epoch's Providence is quite worn out,
The lion of Nothing chases about.

                              (Christmas 1940)

Once more, the ordinary universe of massacres can be only tenuously related to the sense of collapse: the war is experienced, not primarily as concrete action, but as 'This massive vagueness'. Yet the sense of that vagueness then leads, not to a sensitive exploration of the complex patterns of feeling underlying the visible history, but to a sterile dealing in abstractions:

'Beware! Beware! The Great Boyg has you down',
Some deeper instinct in revulsion cries,
'The Void desires to have you for its creature,
A doll through whom It may ventriloquise
Its vast resentment as your very own,
Because Negation has nor form nor feature,
And all Its lust to power is impotent
Unless the actual It hates consents.'

The vagueness, evidently enough, is a quality of the poem's response as much as of its subject-matter. 'The Great Boyg' is of course, a characteristically flippant flirtation with a half-serious notion, but the image is common enough in Auden's poetry to be noted: actual history is merely the superstructural expression of incomprehensibly abstract forces beyond man himself:

We are lived by powers we pretend to understand:
They arrange our loves; it is they who direct at the end
The enemy bullet, the sickness, or even our hand.
                              (*In Memory of Ernst Toller*)

Here, the detail of personal living, like the 'strands of private
order' of *Christmas 1940*, are reduced, rather than opposed, to
the deeper forces of disturbance, but the two attitudes are part
of the same way of looking. In the face of these obscure general
powers, specific detail is seen as either abolished or extraneous.

In several of his shorter poems, Auden returns to the problem
of relating the specifiable facts of individual or social living to
the less tangibly local forces and issues confronting English
culture. The relation of the individual tyrant to his society—

When he laughed, respectable senators burst with laughter,
And when he cried the little children died in the streets
                              (*Epitaph On A Tyrant*)

—has a formal directness and simplicity for which contemporary parallels can be found, but now with a sense of both connection and disjunction:

As evening fell the day's oppression lifted;
Far peaks came into focus; it had rained,
Across wide lawns and cultured flowers drifted
The conversation of the highly trained.

Two gardeners watched them pass and priced their shoes,
A chauffeur waited, reading in the drive,
For them to finish their exchange of views;
It seemed a picture of the private life.

Far off, no matter what good they intended,
The armies waited for a verbal error
With all the instruments for causing pain:

And on the issue of their charm depended
A land laid waste, with all its young men slain,
Its women weeping, and the towns in terror.
                              (*Embassy*)

The link between civilised talk at home and human devastation abroad is dramatically immediate, but its very immediacy exposes the absurd disjunction (and the possibility of erroneous translation) between the two realms. There is a similar paradox at work in *Gare du Midi*:

> *A nondescript express in from the South,*
> *Crowds round the ticket barrier, a face*
> *To welcome which the mayor has not contrived*
> *Bugles or braid: something about the mouth*
> *Distracts the stray look with alarm and pity.*
> *Snow is falling. Clutching a little case,*
> *He walks out briskly to infect a city*
> *Whose terrible future may have just arrived.*

The nondescript triviality of the arrival is menacingly disproportionate to its cataclysmic effect: the routine local details of weather and facial expression obscure the shape of a general disaster which nevertheless lies immediately beneath their surface. The verb which connects general and particular is, significantly, 'infects', which suggests a specific contemporary fear of germ-warfare, but also recalls an image common in Auden:

> *The sinister tall-hatted botanist stoops at the spring*
> *With his insignificant phial and looses*
> *The plague on the ignorant town.*
>
> (*Our City*)

The plague is all-pervading, but it cannot be seen: it suggests an atmosphere of evil too widespread for analysis, too self-generating for control. As an image of war, the plague relates to the 'massive vagueness', at once insistent and elusive, of a 'metaphysical' process beyond individual understanding:

> *Waves of anger and fear*
> *Circulate over the bright*
> *And darkened lands of the earth,*
> *Obsessing our private lives;*
> *The unmentionable odour of death*
> *Offends the September night.*
>
> (*1st September 1939*)

In *Dover 1937*, Auden considers the problem of relating domestic particular to alien generality in explicitly geographical terms: in a contrast between English society and what lies beyond it. For this purpose, Dover is an exact image: on the one hand a settled piece of English culture, on the other hand an entry-point to the unknown:

> . . . *Here live the experts on what the soldiers want*
>   *And who the travellers are,*
> *Whom the ships carry in and out between the lighthouses*
> *That guard for ever the made privacy of this bay*
> *Like twin stone dogs opposed on a gentleman's gate:*
> *Within these breakwaters English is spoken; without*
>   *Is the immense improbable atlas.*

The 'made privacy' of Dover, its insular artifice, is satirised: a previous stanza tells us that 'all this show / Has, somewhere inland, a vague and dirty root'; yet that satire must be balanced, not only against the characteristically English gesture to 'the immense *improbable* atlas' (which shares in, even as it pokes fun at, a provincial outlook), but also against the whimsy of the following stanza:

> *The eyes of the departing migrants are fixed on the sea,*
> *To conjure their special fates from the impersonal water,*
> *'I see an important decision made on a lake,*
> *An illness, a beard, Arabia found in a bed,*
>   *Nanny defeated, Money'.*

The migrants' pathetic expectations are 'placed' as trivial, but the same satirical tone is then extended to those returning home:

> *And filled with the tears of the beaten or calm with fame,*
> *The eyes of the returning thank the historical cliffs,*
> *'The heart has at last ceased to lie, and the clock to accuse;*
> *In the shadow under the yew, at the children's party*
>   *Everything will be explained'.*

Both England and its foreign alternatives sustain illusions: and the poem's attitude to Dover, where these illusions interlock, is correspondingly ambivalent:

> *And the old town with its keep and its Georgian houses*
> *Has built its routine upon these unusual moments;*
> *The vows, the tears, the slight emotional signals*
> *Are here eternal and unremarkable gestures*
>   *Like ploughing or soldiers' songs:*

> *Soldiers who swarm in the pubs in their pretty clothes,*
> *As fresh and silly as girls from a high-class academy:*
> *The Lion, the Rose or the Crown will not ask them to die,*
> *Not here, not now. All they are killing is time,*
>   *Their pauper civilian future.*

Dover has 'built its routine upon these unusual moments': it combines, as a place, those settled particulars of common domestic life, and those echoes of a deeper experience, which we have seen as dislocated elements elsewhere in Auden's poetry. The gestures which typify it are 'eternal', but also 'unremarkable': like ploughing or soldiers' songs, they fuse an ordinary and traditional rhythm with a more profound level of feeling. That ordinariness is then both patronised (the 'fresh and silly' soldiers in 'pretty' clothes) and appreciated as a defence against destruction ('The Lion, the Rose or the Crown will not ask them to die'): England is trivial and tedious, but the alternatives are sinister:

> *Above them, expensive and lovely as a child's toy,*
> *The aeroplanes fly in the new European air,*
> *On the edge of that air that makes England of minor importance;*
> *And the tides warn bronzing bathers of a cooling star,*
>   *With half its history done.*

> *High over France the full moon, cold and exciting*
> *Like one of those dangerous flatterers one meets and loves*
> *When one is very unhappy, returns the human stare:*
> *The night has many recruits; for thousands of pilgrims*
>   *The Mecca is coldness of heart.*

To look beyond the edges of England is to know its pettiness, but also to confront a disorientating vision of general collapse —an image of planetary ruin which can be related to the particulars of Dover life only through the mediating device of the tides, which are at once local and global. In a parallel way, England and France can be linked only by the moon, which is visible to both: natural objects take the full pressure of a relationship which is less easy to establish at the level of human experience.

A crux of the general difficulty we have traced in some of Auden's poems occurs in his *In Memory of W. B. Yeats*: not only as theme, but as a problem of poetic tone. The poem really divides into two sections: the first in Auden's own most typical manner, the second in a metre which recalls that of Yeats himself. This second part attempts a grave, poised, reflective generalisation of the poet's task:

> *Follow, poet, follow right*
> *To the bottom of the night,*
> *With your unconstraining voice*
> *Still persuade us to rejoice. . . .*
>
> *In the deserts of the heart*
> *Let the healing fountain start,*
> *In the prison of his days*
> *Teach the free man how to praise.*

The problem is to square this affirmative lyric with what has gone before, in Auden's more familiar style:

> *. . . For poetry makes nothing happen: it survives*
> *In the valley of its saying where executives*
> *Would never want to tamper. . . .*

The position is not quite self-contradictory, since 'happen' evidently excludes such events as inward healing and rejoicing; but the ambiguity of this attitude towards poetry and society,

where poetry is being seen as at once central and impotent,
relates to an ambiguity surrounding the description of Yeats's
death:

> He disappeared in the dead of winter:
> The brooks were frozen, the airports almost deserted,
> And snow disfigured the public statues;
> The mercury sank in the mouth of the dying day.
> What instruments we have agree
> The day of his death was a dark cold day.

> Far from his illness
> The wolves ran on through the evergreen forests,
> The peasant river was untempted by the fashionable quays;
> By mourning tongues
> The death of the poet was kept from his poems.

The point of this second stanza is to assert the unchanging
normality of life, which the poet's death has not touched; and
it is for this reason that there is such a curious hesitation in
the opening stanza between fact and metaphor. What are
really contingent facts—the frozen brooks, deserted airports,
disfigured statues—are forced by a self-consciously synthetic
process into organic metaphor: and the point of the self-
consciousness is to keep before our minds the arbitrariness of
connection between extraordinary event and quotidian context. 'What instruments we have agree / The day of his death was
a dark cold day' is both solemn rhetoric and deliberate irony:
the weather may indeed have been dark and cold, but the in-
trusive neutrality of 'instruments' points as much to gratuitous
coincidence as to Nature's mourning involvement in the event.
The incongruity is later sharpened:

> . . . A few thousand will think of this day
> As one thinks of a day when one did something slightly
>   unusual.
> What instruments we have agree
> The day of his death was a dark cold day.

The elegy is grave, but it has an inescapable hint of Auden's 'brilliant' frivolousness:

> *Let aeroplanes circle moaning overhead*
> *Scribbling on the sky the message He Is Dead,*
> *Put crêpe bows round the white necks of the public doves,*
> *Let the traffic policemen wear black cotton gloves.*
>
> *(Two Songs for Hedli Anderson)*

Poetry, like the suffering of *Musée des Beaux Arts*, is at once the most intense and most peripheral social fact, but this disjunction of the normal and extraordinary is not especially regretted. If it is true that executives do not 'tamper' with poetry, the force of that verb suggests, perhaps, that Auden is glad enough that they don't.

The problem which I have isolated in some of Auden's early poetry has a direct relevance to the theme of this study. During a period of disintegration, Auden became a spokesman for English society, adopting in this culture a role in many ways similar to the function fulfilled by Yeats in Ireland. Yet the 'totalisation' which that role demanded—the capacity to pose personal feeling and public event, local detail and general vision, in mutually illuminating relation—was one which Auden never really achieved. Because he had both a highly developed talent for abstract generalisation and a remarkably quick eye for the 'telling' detail, he could often enough give the impression of having achieved it; but for most of the time it was never more than a matter of technique. At its worst, Auden's poetry sounds like a kind of parody of a complete vision—a mechanical combination of trivialising particular and glib generalisation:

> *Knowledge of their colonial suffering has cut off*
> *The Hundred Families like an attack of shyness. . . .*
>
> *In the Far West, in absolutely free America,*
> *In melancholy Hungary, and clever France*
> *Where ridicule has acted an important role. . . .*
>
> *(In Time of War, Commentary)*

In better poems, Auden could surmount this glibness; but he could never successfully surmount the fact that he was, despite his Marxism, an essentially 'domestic' poet, deeply shaped by some of the most characteristic ways of seeing of the society he rejected, who tried to grapple with forces and issues beyond this domestic arena.

CHAPTER VII

D. H. Lawrence

I

THERE is a sense in which the problems delineated in this study converge into focus in the life and work of a single twentieth-century writer: D. H. Lawrence. That Lawrence was an exile from his own culture—in some ways, indeed, the archetypal modern exile—is well enough known; the rootless, frustrated wanderings in Europe, America, Australia, New Mexico have been sufficiently documented for that image (translated, often enough, into the distorting terms of a Byronic Romanticism) to have established itself in the general consciousness. But the nature of Lawrence's exile from his own society runs deeper than this. In previous writers, we have seen forms of estrangement from English culture which arose from a simple externality, at crucial points, to the character of its common experience; we have also seen, most evidently in Orwell and Greene, the impotent passivity of the man trapped as a social exile within a culture which could not be escaped, a form of life too oppressively familiar to be surmounted. But neither description fits Lawrence at all exactly. Lawrence's achievement, as both man and writer, was to fight his way free from a repressive society by a route which, in his best work, involved no loss of inwardness with that determining social reality: it is in this that he is genuinely unique.

In his comment on Lawrence in *Culture and Society 1780–1950*, Raymond Williams has valuably emphasised the quality of his personal involvement, from the inside, with the culture he was to grasp, in his mature work, as a complete structure:

> . . . his first social responses were those, not of a man observing the processes of industrialism, but of one caught in them, at an

exposed point, and destined, in the normal course, to be enlisted
in their regiments. That he escaped enlistment is now so well
known to us that it is difficult to realise the thing as it happened, in its living sequence. It is only by hard fighting, and
further, by the fortune of fighting on a favourable front, that
anyone born into the industrial working class escapes his function of replacement. Lawrence could not be certain, at the time
when his fundamental social responses were forming, that he
could so escape.[1]

Lawrence escaped enlistment, but not by the route which
society conventionally offered men in his position: an extrication from the working class for the purposes of recruitment
into the ranks of those who kept them in their place. This was
not simply a matter of 'class-loyalty': it was that what Lawrence
learnt from his childhood experience in a working-class family
included, implicitly and persistently, an education in values and
feelings which were themselves a continuous, often unconscious critique of that dominative middle-class mode. It was
not that the working-class family provided a complete, alternative form of life to the orthodox society: not only because the
ways of feeling it offered were always too close and immediate
to be easily formulated into an alternative ethic, but because
the home, and the whole working-class environment, had its
share of a violence and domination which tied it to the entire
society. The violence of Walter Morel in *Sons and Lovers* repro-
duces, clearly enough, the structure of the dominative society
he serves: the imperious relation of the miner to his wife and
children was for the young Lawrence the most evident point
at which the harsh pressures of the working world entered,
and disrupted, the family settlement. The angry, defensive
gathering of the Morel children around the mother, in opposition to the brutality of the father, is not (as it might be in
a middle-class setting) a matter of family temperaments or
loyalties alone: it is a matter of a conflict and estrangement
which reaches through the family context into the deeper
alternatives of work and personal relationship, selfish individu-

[1] London, 1958, p. 202.

alism and solidarity, mechanical demand and moral sensitivity.

Yet Morel is not only seen as 'outside' the family context, as an alien intruder from the mines: he is also, and equally, a member of the family, who, both on human and economic terms, cannot be denied. It is this which is recognised by Mrs Morel, against her children's angry calls to shut the father out. The father cannot be shut out because he is the provider who holds the family physically together, the man whom Paul and the other children despise yet on whom they are radically dependent. It is for this reason that Paul's own childhood efforts to exclude the world of the father and centre instead on the mother imply a dividing of life and labour which is at once understandable and ultimately false: his hatred of the pit office where he has to collect Morel's wages must be rebuked by his mother, as a dangerously privileged hypersensitivity:

> 'They're hateful, and common, and hateful, they are, and I'm not going any more. Mr Braithwaite drops his "h's", an' Mr Winterbottom says "You was".'
> 'And is that why you won't go any more?' smiled Mrs Morel.
> The boy was silent for some time. His face was pale, his eyes dark and furious. His mother moved about at her work, taking no notice of him. . . . His ridiculous hypersensitivity made her heart ache.

Mrs Morel herself, the 'superior' daughter of an engineering foreman, has had to train herself to the adjustments of feeling which Paul experiences as degrading; and the adjustment is seen not only as a necessity, but as a whole and in some ways valuable way of living. The worlds of human relationship and industrial labour are separate and conflicting, but the separation must not simply be ratified: the conflicts must be fought out within a shared area of living—the family itself. It is within the family, where work and relationship converge, that the essential interactions of both structures of feeling must be seen: not as a simple alternative of colliery and home, but as an interrelation of elements within a single texture of life, where each acts on and modifies the other. Morel brings into the home the callous individualism of a wider society, but he also brings qualities which the mother cannot give: his quick, practical knowledge and vigour:

> The only times when he entered again into the life of his own people was when he worked, and was happy at work. Sometimes, in the evening, he cobbled the boots or mended the kettle of his pit-bottle. Then he always wanted several attendants, and the children enjoyed it. They united with him in the work, in the actual doing of something, when he was his real self again.
>
> He was a good workman, dexterous, and one who, when he was in a good humour, always sang. He had whole periods, months, almost years, of friction and nasty temper. Then sometimes he was jolly again. It was nice to see him run with a piece of red-hot iron into the scullery, crying:
>
> 'Out of my road—out of my road!'

When Morel can make living contact with his children, it is through this kind of immediate, material knowledge: through qualities directly connected with his life as a working man. And it is, to that extent, a fertilising contact—a bringing to bear of a range of experience beyond the home on the family relationships, which must be set against the losses of his selfishness and bad temper. It is not that Morel can be happy as a father and not as a workman, in some simple counterpoising of the two: the point, in a more subtle blending of home and work, is that his 'real', working self can come alive in a family context of free, rather than compulsory, labour.

Morel's selfishness is irresponsible; but it is also the stubborn resistance of a way of life able to exist on its own, immediately sensuous terms, to a kind of moral forcing:

> (Mrs Morel) fought to make him undertake his own responsibilities, to make him fulfil his obligations. But he was too different from her. His nature was purely sensuous, and she strove to make him moral, religious. She tried to force him to face things. He could not endure it—it drove him out of his mind.

It is the balance of sympathy which Lawrence is able to achieve between Morel and his wife which is most impressive. Morel's fecklessness is a serious defect: it is portrayed as an almost animal allegiance to the settled rhythms of an established life-form which damagingly frustrates the possibility of transcendence: of extension, understanding, control. That transcendence, as usual in Lawrence, is symbolised by the woman: but it is too close, as it is presented here, to aspects of an essentially middle-class effort towards 'moral improvement' for it to be wholly approved. Lawrence understands, as many middle-class observers would not, that Morel's sullen obstinacy is more than animal stupidity: it is also the reflex habit of a long defensive tradition, developed by the English working class as a protection against patronage and manipulation from outside.

The strengths and weaknesses of that rooted tradition are, as a matter of general history, almost inextricably linked, and there is a sense in which that inseparability, understood as an experience rather than an analysis, is the subject-matter of *Sons and Lovers*. What is most interesting about the novel is that settlement and transcendence—the instinctive allegiance to a working-class culture and the exploratory movement beyond it—are no more mechanically separable, despite their evident conflict, than the equally conflicting priorities of work and home. Morel moves within the close, restricted limits of a routine working life, instinctively hostile to change and extension; yet that life traditionally includes a margin of free autonomy which is jealously guarded: the right, after work, to the independence of the pub or the day's outing with a mate. What thwarts that welcome release from constraint is the family. The family, ideally a reserve of that freedom and permanent relationship absent at work (where labour is forced and relationships can be broken at any point by dismissal or redundancy), is in fact experienced as a new set of limiting duties and demanding pressures after the work-discipline has been thankfully left behind. It is here that the abstract duality of compulsory labour and free family leisure really breaks down, and the interpenetration of home and work is felt at its most acute. For the working man, the most tangible relation between work and home is the fact of poverty: poverty is the way in which the paucity of a working-life registers itself in the constraints of a family context. For the middle-class man, there may be an escape from a demanding work-discipline to the relaxed privacy of family life, but no such escape is open to a man like Morel. It is not only that the work-discipline is harsher, and the energy for recreation therefore less available, nor even that the boundaries between public work and private home-life are less strict, in a community of families united by the same working experience; it is that relaxation in a home permanently beset by human and financial anxieties rooted in the character of the work itself is almost impossible. Lawrence understood this thoroughly, and it is on this basis, rather than on some patronising admiration for 'animal vigour', that his sympathy with Morel rests. As the novel progresses, Morel is reduced to a shrunken, almost broken man, and this is in part a function of the novel's own shifting focus, as the immediate working environment recedes into the background and Paul's own venture into consciousness begins to predominate. Yet it is also important to see that what deprives Morel of manhood is not only this changing perspective, and not primarily the brutal disciplines of industrial capitalism, but the shaming consciousness of his failure to shoulder the burden of family life. Morel can survive the rigours of work, not only because he has the necessary physical strength, but because he clings to his narrow margin of freedom and retains from his youth a sensuous capacity to live for the present which inures him to the taxing demands of the pit. Yet these, precisely, are among the reasons which unfit him for family responsibility: the qualities essential to survive the world of work become the qualities which destroy his capacity for responsible relationship in the home. The fecklessness of Morel the miner, bred at least in part by a system of work which requires of him not human responsibility but mere physical expenditure, becomes the selfishness of Morel the husband and father, able to involve himself with his children only by his practical skills.

Morel, then, does not merely represent a narrow settlement which must be gone beyond: he symbolises also a stubbornly asserted independence of the ties of family which is in one sense destructive, in another sense an aspect of traditional masculinity which Paul himself is unable to achieve. There is a similar ambivalence in the portrayal of Mrs Morel. Mrs Morel is the central life-source of the family, and the bond which ties Paul to her, in an intense inwardness, ties him also to the working-class childhood culture of which she is symbol. But she is also, like the farmwomen of *The Rainbow*, the point which opens into a dimension beyond that immediate world: she represents an impulse within the traditional settlement for extension and transcendence. That transcendence, of course, will happen not through her own life but through Paul's, who is not to follow his father into the colliery. Yet the tension which this situation then involves is that the movement towards transcendence to a wider life springs from the very centre of the traditional culture: Mrs Morel is symbol both of that culture at its most positive, and of a striving towards the new. The result, in the relationship between her and Paul, is a complex irony. Paul, as his mother's child, moves beyond the boundaries of the family into a wider world; yet the force which impels him there—his mother's influence—is also the force which draws him irresistibly back home. For her part, Mrs Morel is determined that Paul should escape the colliery, but the love which motivates that choice is also unable to release him from its control into the desired life of developed consciousness and autonomous relationship. The result is then a deadlock: Paul can neither escape from his old environment into a new dimension nor re-enter its life on the old terms. He can reject Mrs Morel's possessiveness in the person of Miriam, yet the rejection of Miriam, paradoxically, is an option for his mother.

It is that option for his mother which inhibits Paul's

independence; yet what independence he has is, ironically, an almost exact reproduction of the shifting instability of his father:

> Morel sat down. Both the men seemed helpless, and each of them had a rather hunted look. But Dawes now carried himself quietly, seemed to yield himself, while Paul seemed to screw himself up. Clara thought she had never seen him look so small and mean. He was as if trying to get himself into the smallest possible compass. . . . Watching him unknown, she said to herself there was no stability about him. He was fine in his way, passionate, and able to give her drinks of pure life when he was in one mood. And now he looked paltry and insignificant. There was nothing stable about him. Her husband had more manly dignity. At any rate *he* did not waft about with any wind. There was something evanescent about Morel, she thought, something shifting and false. He would never make sure ground for any woman to stand on.

The irony of Paul's condition is that freedom and rootedness are not really opposed feelings: on the contrary, it is because what rootedness he has known is so abnormally intense that the break beyond it can only take the form of an equally flawed restlessness. Paul's 'evanescent' mobility of spirit is not a clear alternative to the settled family culture, as his brother William's is; it is rather the reaction of a man who resents that culture's paralysing grip on his life but is unable to break free, the self-consuming motion of a man bound tight to what he struggles against.

Sons and Lovers is Lawrence's first major exploration of the problem of a man's relation to his own culture, and it is, of course, tentative and uncertain in its final attitude. At the level of explicit content, in the history of Paul Morel, it remains too deeply inward with the felt reality of working-class life for the movement beyond that world to be more than a confused sense of fumbling; yet it is precisely in the written depth and intricacy of that inwardness, in the marvellously rendered interior detail of family life, that Lawrence's own partial transcendence of the limits still constraining Paul reveals itself. It is not that Lawrence has moved beyond that life to a vantage-point from which it can be externally 'placed': for it was an aspect both of his integrity and his tragedy, as a man, that he recognised that, once that life was lost, there was nowhere else to move. The orthodox alternative—an enlistment in the middle class—hardly needed to be tried: for the sensitive working-class child, as Paul shows, can learn the essentials of that ideology, in the conditions of his own people, without moving from home. Nor is the 'placing' of those conditions achieved, in this novel, through 'ideas': Paul's irritation with Miriam's passionately abstract intensities springs in part from a sense that they falsify more tangible realities. The placing is achieved, not through 'spiritual' reflection, but through the qualities of writing in which the working-class world comes to life—qualities which contain their own organising evaluations:

> He jerked at the drawer in his excitement. It fell, cut sharply on his shin, and on the reflex he flung it at her.
> One of the corners caught her brow as the shallow drawer crashed into the fireplace. She swayed, almost fell stunned from her chair. To her very soul she was sick; she clasped the child tightly to her bosom. A few moments elapsed; then, with an effort, she brought herself to. The baby was crying plaintively. Her left brow was bleeding rather profusely. As she glanced down at the child, her brain reeling, some drops of blood soaked into its white shawl; but the baby was at least not hurt. She balanced her head to keep equilibrium, so that the blood ran into her eye.
> Walter Morel remained as he had stood, leaning on the table with one hand, looking blank. When he was sufficiently sure of his balance, he went across to her, swayed, caught hold of the back of her rocking-chair, almost tipping her out; then, leaning forward over her, and swaying as he spoke, he said, in a tone of wondering concern:
> 'Did it catch thee?'
> . . . 'Go away,' she said, struggling to keep her presence of mind.
> He hiccoughed. 'Let's—let's look at it,' he said, hiccoughing again.

What is most impressive about this passage, enforcing as it does the unbalanced violence of Morel, is its refusal to surrender at any point to stock notions of lower-class brawling. The emotional crisis is acute, and the blood on the baby's shawl tactfully symbolic, but most of the attention is directed to the detail of bodily movement and the practical necessities of guarding the child from harm: of preserving physical, as much as personal, balance. It is through these quite physical terms that the essential judgements on both Morel and his wife are communicated: the father's fumbling, self-defeating, inarticulate uncertainty, which makes for both cruelty and tenderness; the mother's driving impulse to hold the family physically together, to subdue her own feeling to material necessity in a curt, practical coldness at once essential and estranging. It is in what is not said, by both Lawrence and his characters, and how it is not said, that the significance of the incident emerges.

In the pattern of *Sons and Lovers*, the rhythm of inwardness and externality to a culture expresses itself as a rhythm of successive generations. In the unfolding of a family history, each generation is tied by interior bonds to its parents and yet is external, even alien, to them; and it is this rich paradox which Lawrence exploits to furnish himself with a total structure for *The Rainbow*. Each settlement offers a source of life to its children, but in a continuity of conflict rather than of simple extension: the offered life must be accepted, but accepted in a way which, by gathering it into a movement of transcendence, seems also a denial of its terms. That sense of transcendence is the novel's opening emphasis, in the contrast between the men and women of a single generation:

> But the woman wanted another form of life than this, something that was not blood-intimacy. Her house faced out from the farm-buildings and fields, looked out to the road and village with church and Hall and the world beyond. She stood to see the far-off world of cities and governments and the active scope of man, the magic land to her, where secrets were made known and desires fulfilled. She faced outwards to where men moved dominant and creative, having turned their back on the pulsing

heat of creation, and with this behind them, were set out to
discover what was beyond, to enlarge their own scope and
range and freedom; whereas the Brangwen men faced inwards
to the teeming life of creation, which poured unresolved into
their veins.

The men who turn outwards to the beyond turn their backs
on the rich fertility of the known life, but it is 'behind them' in
a figurative as well as a literal sense: the old culture is broken
with, but continues to sustain. In the early chapters of the novel,
the sense of that transcendent realm enters Tom Brangwen's
world: first through the foreigner he meets at Matlock, then
through his wife Lydia. The foreigner rouses in Brangwen a
radical discontent with his established life: 'He baulked the
mean enclosure of reality, stood stubbornly like a bull at the
gate, refusing to re-enter the well-known round of his own
life . . . He wanted to go away—right away. He dreamed of
foreign parts. But somehow he had no contact with them. And
it was a very strong root which held him to the Marsh, to his
own house and land.' The tension here, between the tie to a
traditional culture and a restlessness which impels Brangwen
beyond its frontiers, is very close in quality to the problem
which confronted Paul Morel; yet Brangwen's marriage to
Lydia offers a kind of temporary solution. What is remarkable
about *The Rainbow* is the way in which the question of balance
between relatedness and autonomy, between the acceptance
and surmounting of a particular context, is at once a cultural
issue—the problem of attaining the right tension of intimacy
and externality between generations, or between home and
'foreign' experience—and yet registers itself directly in the
quality and movement of specific relationships. Those relationships emerge from, and help to shape, the deeper issues of
cultural identity; and it is for this reason that Brangwen, in
taking as his wife a woman who is at once mysteriously alien
('It was to him a profound satisfaction that she was a foreigner')
and yet intuitively inward with the life of the Marsh, can reach
a kind of fulfilment.

As the novel progresses, that kind of fulfilling balance becomes increasingly difficult to achieve. The 'mean enclosure' of quotidian reality can be re-created, for Brangwen, by the gathering of a transcendent mystery to its centre; but as the pressures of an impoverished society are taken, that movement towards transcendence, for want of an adequate cultural realisation, begins to turn in on itself, in an affirmation of passionate inwardness over against a public culture which now seems increasingly external. 'Transcendence' still finds a meaning within the unfolding, generational rhythm of an historical progress towards freedom, but its most obvious symbolism now carries a different reference, to a timeless moment of interior triumph over history and culture themselves:

> And yet, for his own part, for his private being, (Will) Brangwen felt that the whole of the man's world was exterior and extraneous to his own real life with Anna. Sweep away the whole monstrous superstructure of the world of today, cities and industries and civilisation, leave only the bare earth with plants growing and waters running, and he would not mind, so long as he were whole, had Anna and the child and the new, strange certainty in his soul.

This affirmative extrication from a public history repeats itself later, in Ursula's exultation with Skrebensky:

> During the next weeks, all the time she went about in the same dark richness, her eyes dilated and shining like the eyes of a wild animal, a curious half-smile which seemed to be gibing at the civic pretence of all the human life about her.
> 'What are you, you pale citizens?' her face seemed to say, gleaming. 'You subdued beast in sheep's clothing, you primeval darkness falsified to a social mechanism.'
> She went about in the sensual sub-consciousness all the time, mocking at the ready-made, artificial day-light of the rest.

It is important to note this shift of meaning in 'transcendence' in *The Rainbow*, as it points forward to some of Lawrence's later attitudes, most evidently in *Women in Love*. Ursula's response is not wholly endorsed—it is described as a 'dark sensual arrogance', which cannot in any case be detached from its specific context in her spiritual history—but it is, nevertheless, a response which catches up, in its dualistic antitheses of passion and consciousness, authenticity and 'mere' social mechanism, person and public history, a significant range of Lawrence's own more questionable values. To say this is not merely to score a local point against Lawrence, but to notice what happens, almost inevitably, to the search for transcendence in a society which in practice denies its general and concrete realisation. *The Rainbow*, more obviously than *Sons and Lovers*, is able to grasp the interior connections between particular relationships and the shape of a common history: not only in the local context of the Marsh farm, where these are tangibly interwoven in the life of a working generation, but (a much more difficult recognition) in English society as a whole. In the development of Ursula—her teaching, her relations with Skrebensky and Winifred Inger—a whole social structure of feeling is projected, relating specific histories to the outlines of an entire culture in a way which was not on the whole possible in *Sons and Lovers*. A totalisation, of a kind, is achieved, without damage to the specificity of the inward and personal; yet it is important to see, as the above quotations indicate, that the relation of persons and society is as much one of contrast as of continuity. In one sense, of course, this is the whole of Lawrence's point: it is precisely in the telling opposition between the creative potency of individual lives, and the dehumanised mechanism of a dominative society, that the necessary social judgement is made to emerge. But this sensitive evaluation can be felt as interacting with a less flexibly intelligent model: the dualistic notion of an inwardly authentic spontaneity set over against a merely 'external' society which Lawrence inherited from nineteenth-century vitalism and idealism, and which was always deeply lodged in his thinking. When this model is dominant, it is not a particular society, but society itself, which deadens and falsifies; and the sense of a culture's externality to its members then becomes less the fruit of sensitive perception than the reflex response of a stereotype.

Yet it is a measure of *The Rainbow*'s fine achievement that it does not, on the whole, surrender too readily to this stereotype in its actual writing. An interesting illustration is the encounter between Ursula and the family on the barge:

> They had walked till they had reached a wharf, just above a lock. There an empty barge, painted with a red and yellow cabin hood, was lying moored. A man, lean and grimy, was sitting on a box against the cabin-side by the door, smoking, and nursing a baby that was wrapped in a drab shawl. . . .
>
> 'Good evening,' he called, half impudent, half attracted. He had blue eyes which glanced impudently from his grimy face. . . .
>
> 'May I look inside your barge?' asked Ursula.
>
> 'There's nobody to stop you; you come if you like. . . .'
>
> Ursula peeped into the cabin, where saucepans were boiling and some dishes were on the table. It was very hot. Then she came out again. The man was talking to the baby. It was a blue-eyed, fresh-faced thing with floss of red-gold hair. . . .

Ursula, captivated by the child, offers the father her necklace to give to it:

> The jewel swung from the baby's hand and fell in a little heap on the coal-dusty bottom of the barge. The man groped for it, with a kind of careful reverence. Ursula noticed the coarsened, blunted fingers groping at the little jewelled heap. The skin was red on the back of the hand, the fair hairs glistened stiffly. It was a thin, sinewy, capable hand nevertheless, and Ursula liked it. He took up the necklace, carefully, and blew the coal-dust from it, as it lay in the hollow of his hand. He seemed still and attentive. He held out his hand with the necklace shining small in its hard, black hollow.
>
> 'Take it back,' he said.
>
> Ursula hardened with a kind of radiance.
>
> 'No,' she said. 'It belongs to little Ursula. . . .'
>
> There was a moment of confusion, then the father bent over his child:
>
> 'What do you say?' he said. 'Do you say thank you? Do you say thank you, Ursula?'

'Her name's Ursula *now*,' said the mother, smiling a little bit
ingratiatingly from the door. . . .
The father looked up at (Ursula) with an intimate, half-
gallant, half-impudent, but wistful look. His captive soul loved
her: but his soul was captive, he knew, always. . . .
Ursula joined Skrebensky. . . .
'I *loved* them,' she was saying. 'He was so gentle—oh, so
gentle! And the baby was such a dear!'
'Was he gentle?' said Skrebensky. 'The woman had been a
servant, I'm sure of that.'

There is enough externality in the passage's attitude to the
working-class family to enforce a significant contrast with the
treatment of the Morels': Ursula, ironically, is here in something like the position of Lily in *Sons and Lovers*, the refined
young girl whom William brings home to survey the mysteries
of working-class family-life. Lily's attitude was one of con-
descending amusement, which is not, of course, true of Ursula;
yet there is a similarity of viewpoint, all the same, in this passing peep into an excitingly alien world. If Lily's response was
one of amused patronage, Ursula's is one of amused admiration: both, essentially, suggest the attitude of an observer,
briefly enjoying an environment which does not have to be
permanently lived in, and no doubt enjoying it all the more for
that. The texture of detailed description, in contrast with *Sons
and Lovers*, is thin, and there is an alert awareness of 'impudence'
and 'ingratiation', qualifying the vitality, which is again very
much a middle-class attitude. Yet Lawrence's intimate feel for
creative life is still sharp: the working man and his wife are
hardly realised in any full way, but there is enough felt tenderness, even so, to show up the stiffness of Skrebensky, and the
ideology he embodies, for what it is. That revelation is not
simple: Ursula's action displays a generosity of spirit beyond
Skrebensky, but a sense of its potential self-indulgence—its
lavish offensiveness to the necessarily reserved and guarded
thrift of the bargeman—is also communicated, to complicate
judgement. The deepest moral insight is then the bargeman's
capacity, in response to Ursula's openness, consciously to

break with his settled habits, in a movement of reciprocation. Both he and Ursula, in contrast with Skrebensky, are able to recognise, and respond to, an event which transcends the limits of their habitual situations.

Ursula, then, has moved beyond her childhood culture, but she is still able to establish living connection with it; and it is this balance, between the more complete version of society possible to developed consciousness, and a preserved respect for its particular life, which is captured in the rhetoric of *The Rainbow*'s final passage:

> She saw the stiffened bodies of the colliers, which seemed already enclosed in a coffin, she saw their unchanging eyes, the eyes of those who are buried alive: she saw the hard, cutting edges of the new houses, which seemed to spread over the hill-side in insentient triumph, a triumph of horrible, amorphous angles and straight lines, the expression of corruption triumphant and unopposed, corruption so pure that it is hard and brittle: she saw the dun atmosphere over the blackened hills opposite, the dark blotches of houses, slate roofed and amorphous, the old church-tower standing up in hideous obsoleteness above raw new houses on the crest of the hill, the amorphous, brittle, hard edged new houses advancing from Beldover to meet the corrupt new houses from Lethley, the houses of Lethley advancing to mix with the houses of Hainor, a dry brittle, terrible corruption spreading over the face of the land, and she was sick with a nausea so deep that she perished as she sat. And then, in the blowing clouds, she saw a band of faint iridescence colouring in faint colours a portion of the hill. . . .
>
> And the rainbow stood on the earth. She knew that the sordid people who crept hard-scaled and separate on the face of the world's corruption were living still, that the rainbow was arched in their blood and would quiver to life in their spirit, that they would cast off their horny covering of disintegration, that new, clean, naked bodies would rise to a new germination, to a new growth, rising to the light and the wind and the clean rain of heaven. She saw in the rainbow the earth's new architecture, the old, brittle corruption of houses and factories swept away, the world built up in a living fabric of Truth, fitting to the over-arching heaven.

This, quite evidently, is a 'totalisation' of a direct and unflinch-
ingly explicit kind: an intensely persuasive vision of an entire
culture, sustained by the force of a controlled and intricately
elaborated rhetoric. Yet it is clearly more than an abstract
vision of collapse projected on to a selective pattern of local
detail: the technique, in other words, is not Eliot's. At every
point, generalising judgement is substantiated by the specific:
not simply in the sense that particular perceptions exemplify
an argument or are used to generate one, but in a highly
complex blending and crossing of an actual and a moral landscape, where description and attitude continually combine.
The 'brittleness' and 'hard cutting edges' of the new houses
are both literal and figurative, and so is their uncontrolled
sprawl over the hill-side: on the one hand a metaphor of
spawning corruption, but also a particular network of 'amorphous angles and straight lines', clearly seen and registered. 'A
dry, brittle, terrible corruption' is advancing across the land,
but the terrain of its action is local geography: Beldover,
Lethley, Hainor; 'advancing' is both factually exact, and charged
with a menacing overtone of invasion. The vision is not 'inward', but neither is it Olympian: it totalises and elaborates,
from the distancing standpoint of a solitary observer, a culture
which is nevertheless intimately known. The image of the
rainbow is visionary assertion rather than realistic assessment,
and its specific point of purchase on the preceding description
is disturbingly obscure; yet it captures, through an image of
cultural death and re-creation, that fine tension of conflict and
continuity which throughout the novel has characterised the
interrelationships of persons and generations. The new creation
which the rainbow prefigures is in one sense a decisive rupture
with the diseased present, as the child ruptures the parental
settlement; once contemporary society has been grasped with
this degree of integral awareness, the solution can only be of
such a total and revolutionary kind. Yet the rainbow is also
symbol of what is 'living still', 'arched in the blood' of the
corrupted present: to this extent it affirms both continuity and

inwardness in the context of apocalyptic change. Society must be remade, with a completeness perceptible only to a man free from limiting investments in its present reality; yet it is *this* society which must be remade—these sordid, hard-scaled, separate people, known as they are from the inside. The form of contemporary culture is violently rejected, but within a continuing reverence for the still active energies of its people: and it is this fusion of uncompromising denial and persisting hope which is the passage's most striking quality. The novel's recurrent rhythm of intimacy and estrangement, settlement and transcendence, the spending and re-charging of energies, culminates here in an image of death and resurrection.

II

It is interesting to note the contrast between the stance of *The Rainbow*'s closing passage and the predominant tone of *Women in Love*:

> 'Not many people are anything at all,' (Birkin) answered, forced to go deeper than he wanted to. 'They jingle and giggle. It would be much better if they were just wiped out. Essentially, they don't exist, they aren't there.'

Birkin, of course, does not go entirely uncriticised: but it is significant that what qualifying judgements surround him concern not so much what he says, as the didactic manner in which he says it. If his position is not to be taken as wholly Lawrentian, it is not on account of other viewpoints in the novel which might challenge it: no such alternatives are available. So we are forced to conclude that Birkin's remarks merit serious attention, despite their flavour of contemptuous, neurotic externality posturing as reflective wisdom:

> 'We have an ideal of a perfect world, clean and straight and sufficient. So we cover the earth with foulness; life is a blotch of labour, like insects scurrying in filth, so that your collier can have a pianoforte in his parlour, and you can have a butler

and a motor-car in your up-to-date house, and as a nation we can sport the Ritz, or the Empire, Gaby Deslys and the Sunday newspapers. It is very dreary.'

This is an extension, but also a vulgarisation, of *The Rainbow*'s final vision of decay: the generalised superficiality suggested by this lame collection of cant phrases is now much more a quality of the observer's standpoint than of what is observed. The world, in Birkin's own term, is 'extraneous' to creative individuality; and from this detached, disgusted viewpoint, society can be abstracted to 'mankind', and that in turn abstracted to a petty, ephemeral exhalation of a non-human creative urge:

> 'Let mankind pass away—time it did. The creative utterances will not cease, they will only be there. Humanity doesn't embody the utterance of the incomprehensible any more. Humanity is a dead letter. There will be a new embodiment, in a new way. Let humanity disappear as quickly as possible.'

A new creation is still desired, but it is no longer, as it was in *The Rainbow*, a re-creation. That revolutionary relationship to a culture which *The Rainbow* was able to define, grasping present and future in dialectical interrelation, overbalances here into a blank dislocation between actual and potential. The result is a curious deadlock: a new order must be achieved to replace the present, yet such an attitude already implies, if only negatively, a commitment to the present which is itself restrictive:

> 'I do think,' (Ursula said), 'that one can't have anything new whilst one cares for the old—do you know what I mean?— even fighting the old is belonging to it. I know, one is tempted to stop with the world, just to fight it. But then it isn't worth it.'
> Gudrun considered herself.
> 'Yes,' she said. 'In a way, one is of the world if one lives in it. But isn't it really an illusion to think you can get out of it? After all, a cottage in the Abruzzi, or wherever it may be, isn't a new world. No, the only thing to do with the world, is to see it through.'

The offered alternatives are Ursula's refusal to be bound, even critically, to contemporary society—'even fighting the old is belonging to it'—and Gudrun's tired option for compromise. The problem finds its fullest formulation in the issue of expatriatism:

> 'Oh, of course,' cried Gudrun, 'One could never feel like this in England, for the simple reason that the damper is *never* lifted off one, there. It is quite impossible really to let go, in England, of that I am assured . . . But wouldn't it be wonderful if all England *did* suddenly go off like a display of fireworks.'
> 'It couldn't,' said Ursula. 'They are all too damp, the powder is damp in them.'
> 'I'm not so sure of that,' said Gerald.
> 'Nor I,' said Birkin. 'When the English really begin to go off, *en masse*, it'll be time to shut your ears and run. . . .'
> 'Don't be too hard on poor old England,' said Gerald. 'Though we curse it, we love it really. . . .'
> 'We may,' said Birkin. 'But it's a damnably uncomfortable love: like a love for an aged parent who suffers horribly from a complication of diseases, for which there is no hope. . . .'
> 'Yes,' said Gudrun slowly, 'you love England immensely, *immensely*, Rupert.'

The relationship to England is still a complex fusion of commitment and rejection, but the complexity is now cerebral and asserted, reflected in the banal imagery and brittle feeling of the whole passage; if Birkin does 'love England immensely', it is nowhere shown in the novel. What *is* shown is the despairing vacuity of a particular group of bored middle-class intellectuals, hopelessly alienated from the concrete social realities they analyse at such length.

Gudrun's reaction to the mining community is a useful illustration of this changed relationship to English society:

> They were passing between blocks of miners' dwellings. In the back yards of several dwellings a miner could be seen washing himself in the open on this hot evening, naked down to the loins, his great trousers of moleskin slipping almost away. Miners already cleaned were sitting on their heels, with their backs near the walls, talking and silent in pure physical

well-being, tired, and taking physical rest. Their voices sounded
out with strong intonation, and the broad dialect was curiously
caressing to the blood. It seemed to envelop Gudrun in a labour-
er's caress, there was in the whole atmosphere, a resonance of
physical men, a glamorous thickness of labour and maleness,
surcharged in the air. But it was universal in the district, and
therefore unnoticed by the inhabitants.

To Gudrun, however, it was potent and half-repulsive. She
could never tell why Beldover was so utterly different from
London and the south, why one's whole feelings were different,
why one seemed to live in another sphere. Now she realised
that this was the world of powerful, underworld men who
spent most of their time in the darkness. In their voices she
could hear the voluptuous resonance of darkness, the strong,
dangerous underworld, mindless, inhuman. They sounded
also like strange machines, heavy, oiled. The voluptuousness
was like that of machinery, cold and iron.

It is the confusion of feeling here which is most interesting: the
ambivalent blendings of fascination and disgust. The miners
spread 'a glamorous thickness of labour and maleness' in the
evening air, but their presence to Gudrun is precisely that: an
atmosphere rather than a group of physical men, an hypnotic
pattern of disembodied voices rather than a human conversation. The miners are mysterious, which is the source of both
wonder and revulsion: they are potent and sensuous, but 'the
voluptuousness was like that of machinery, cold and iron'. The
simile is strikingly peculiar: how can a dark, sensual voluptuousness suggest the 'cold and iron' of machinery? The answer
is that the passage is not really attending to the specific qualities
of the miners: it is thinking of the 'dangerous underworld' they
symbolise, which is literally mechanical but metaphorically
dark and potent. Both meanings are forced together in the
simile, but they are really irreconcilable images, springing from
attitudes which conflict rather than interrelate: on the one hand,
a revulsion from what the miners literally represent, but also
an attempt, through metaphor, to endow them with a creative
power alien to Gudrun herself. This forcing of images reveals
the extent to which the whole passage, despite its effort to evoke

a forceful physicality, operates in abstractions: the abstraction, for instance, of connecting the sound of dialect to a physical caress. Physical and moral meanings are subtly maladjusted: a fact which, as we shall see later, is indicative of a more general maladjustment, throughout the novel, between subjective feeling and objective life. The miners 'belong to another world': but while this is at one level part of their attraction for Gudrun, it is at another level what prevents their culture from engaging significantly with her own. The active tension of the earlier novels, between developed consciousness and a working environment, now appears as an unbridgeable rift.

That rift is perhaps most obvious in the scene where Birkin and Ursula give away a chair to a young working-class couple. The incident directly recalls the encounter with the family on the barge in *The Rainbow*, and so can be usefully compared with it:

> 'We wanted to *give* it to you,' explained Ursula, now over-come with confusion and dread of them. She was attracted by the young man. He was a still mindless creature, hardly a man at all, a creature that the towns have produced, strangely pure-bred and fine in one sense, furtive, quick, subtle. . . . His legs would be marvellously subtle and alive, under the shapeless trousers, he had some of the fineness and stillness and silkiness of a dark-eyed silent rat. . . .
> The man jerked his head a little on one side, indicating Ursula, and said, with curious amiable, jeering warmth:
> 'What she warnt?—eh?' An odd smile writhed his lips. . . .
> He was impassive, abstract, like some dark suggestive presence, a gutter presence. . . .
> 'Cawsts something to chynge your mind,' he said in an incredibly low accent.

Ursula finds the youth attractive, as she did the bargeman, but it is now the attractiveness of an animal. His 'dark suggestive presence' is associated, not with a human vitality, but with the 'gutter'; his slowness to respond to the gift is seen, not as the dignified independence of the bargeman, but as a vulgar and calculating suspicion.

It is difficult to see how a novel which supposedly elicits the pattern of feeling of a whole culture, and yet which is as external to its society as this, can really constitute a great achievement; and indeed *Women in Love* seems to me, for this reason, decidedly inferior to both *Sons and Lovers* and *The Rainbow*. It is not a question of 'social realism' against 'symbolism': it is that, whereas the unique strength of the earlier novels sprang in part from the immediate presence of a complex social fabric in which particular relationships were embedded, the narrowing evident in *Women in Love*—the intense focusing on a restricted set of relationships which seem to move in a vacuum—can be directly felt in the attenuated quality of the relationships themselves. There is, of course, a good deal of talk about 'society', but it is, precisely, talk: the vague, abstracted, flippant or earnest philosophising of a self-consciously lost generation. There is the social imagery of the mines; but the mines are not seen, as Ursula's school is seen in *The Rainbow*. And this pervasive thinness of social texture has an immediate effect upon the quality of personal life in the novel. Emotions in *Women in Love* have a curiously overwhelming intensity: there is this reaction of Gudrun's, for instance, to her first sight of Gerald—

> 'His totem is the wolf,' she repeated to herself.
> 'His mother is an old, unbroken wolf.' And then she experienced a keen paroxysm, a transport, as if she had made some incredible discovery, known to nobody else on earth. A strange transport took possession of her, all her veins were in a paroxysm of violent sensation.

—or Hermione's response to Birkin's absence at the church-altar:

> And then, he was not there. A terrible storm came over her, as if she were drowning. She was possessed by a devastating hopelessness. And she approached mechanically to the altar. Never had she known such a pang of utter and final hopelessness. It was beyond death, so utterly null, desert.

In each case (and these are only two, relatively minor instances) feeling becomes abnormally inflated because the capacity adequately to realise its 'objective correlative' in the public world has significantly diminished. The easy traffic between object and response which characterised *Sons and Lovers*, the sense of an objective world existing in its own substantial terms, is now almost entirely lacking. It is confined, essentially, to a few random passages of Nature description, where Lawrence's typifying genius comes momentarily through. The process which we observed in *The Rainbow*, of an inward, self-communing transcendence repelling the crude invasions of 'extraneous' society, culminates here in a dramatic and often wild disproportion between event and response, public culture and private experience.

Between *Women in Love* and *Lady Chatterley's Lover*, Lawrence travelled in Australia and New Mexico, driven from a collapsing England but unable to find an adequate foreign alternative. The effects of that frustrated exploration can be felt in *Lady Chatterley's Lover* in two, ironically conflicting ways: in an increased alienation from English society, and in an increased determination to salvage some positive value from it. Clifford Chatterley is 'frightened of middle and lower class humanity, and of foreigners not of his own class', and Connie can feel 'how little connection he really had with people':

> The miners were, in a sense, his own men; but he saw them as objects rather than men, parts of the pit rather than parts of life, crude raw phenomena rather than human beings along with him.

It is against Clifford's 'nasty, sterile want of common sympathy', his incapacity to establish living relation with others, that Connie revolts; and in that revolt Lawrence's best self, with its memories of a past when miners were relatives and neighbours, can still be felt. But although Clifford's inhumanity is rejected, his actual judgements on the character of working people are still, paradoxically, half-endorsed:

> '. . . in your sense of the word, they are *not* men. They are animals you don't understand, and never could. Don't thrust your

illusions on other people. The masses were always the same, and will always be the same. . . . The masses are unalterable. It is one of the most momentous facts of social science. *Panem et circenses*! Only today education is one of the bad substitutes for a circus. What is wrong today is that we've made a profound hash of the circuses part of the programme, and poisoned our masses with a little education.'

When Clifford became really roused in his feelings about the common people, Connie was frightened. There was something devastatingly true in what he said. But it was a truth that killed.

Clifford's position can be emotionally challenged, but not in a way which can question his intellectual argument. He has been satirised, early in the novel, for his fear of the lesser breeds, but Connie, too, is 'absolutely afraid of the industrial masses':

Perhaps they were only weird fauna of the coal-seams. Creatures of another reality, they were elementals, serving the element of coal, as the metal-workers were elementals, serving the element of iron. Men not men, but animals of coal and iron and clay. Fauna of the elements, carbon, iron, silicon: elementals. . . . They belonged to the coal, the iron, the clay, as fish belong to the sea and worms to dead wood. The anima of mineral disintegration!

The deep alienation implicit in this unreal poetic musing is a constant element in the novel: it must be taken together with Connie's reflection that the affairs of nearby Tevershall 'sounded really more like a Central African jungle than an English village'.

Lawrence is still sufficiently intimate with English society to recognise, as Clifford cannot, that it has important sources of strength; but he is sufficiently exterior, as the returned exile, to share profoundly in Clifford's remote and dehumanising perspective. The problem which the novel poses, then, is how Chatterley's emotional frigidity towards those beyond his class is to be rejected without his particular judgements on their subhuman inferiority being called into radical question; and the answer, in a word, is Mellors. Mellors 'seemed so unlike a game-keeper, so unlike a working-man . . . although he had something in common with the local people. But also something very uncommon.' Mellors, who is working-class Englishman, educated gentleman and mysterious foreigner (he has served in India), is thus the ideal formula for a 'solution': and much of the time, indeed, he is little more than that. Connie, tired of inadequate English lovers, desires a foreigner: 'not an English-man, still less an Irishman. A real foreigner.' Mellors can fulfil this role, since he has lived abroad and is in any case of the alien working class; and since he has that English social background, Connie can satisfy her need for 'foreign' experience by a route which (we are supposed to believe) leads her to the heart of her own culture. In so far as Mellors is working class, Connie's relationship with him provides a living critique of Clifford's snobbery; but in so far as he has moved beyond that class, his be-haviour does not disturb the novel's rigid preconceptions about the 'weird fauna' of the social underworld. Thus, Clifford's belief in dominative class-rule is satirically undermined in the scene where he is forced to accept Mellors's help with his wheel-chair; but since it is Mellors, rather than another, less 'un-common' servant who is there to help, the satire goes against Clifford's personal impotence rather than his political ideology.

The achievement of *Lady Chatterley's Lover* lies in the fact that even here, at this late and radically disillusioned point of Lawrence's career, the sense of those creative potencies which can survive social disintegration is still quick and active. It is a measure of Lawrence's continuing genius that he is able, even at this sterile distance from an actual society, to recognise and re-create its most positive life. Yet this, in the context of the whole work, must be a marginal qualification rather than a general endorsement. As a complete novel, *Lady Chatterley's Lover* fails, and it fails because Lawrence, with his years of root-less exile behind him, is least in touch where he needs to be most incisive: in his feel for the tangible realities of his own society.

III

In a discussion with Ursula in *Women in Love*, Birkin voices a characteristic attitude towards their relationship:

'Don't you see that it's not a question of visual appreciation in the least,' he cried. 'I don't *want* to see you. I've seen plenty of women, I'm sick and weary of seeing them. I want a woman I don't see.'

Birkin's irritable rejection of Ursula's physical presence in his life is one symptom of the deadlock at which Lawrence himself, in his struggle with the problems of settlement and transcendence, finally arrived. Lawrence never relinquished his belief, inherited chiefly from his own working-class experience, that personal fulfilment could be found only in human relationship; but in his fight to break free of relationships which were in practice limiting and restrictive, human contact, and the very existence of others, could seem, at times, a thwarting bondage in itself. Birkin's search is for a relationship which has passed beyond relationship: for a rooted and permanent settlement which offers at the same time the ground of a limitless personal autonomy. *Women in Love* explores that paradox, and the deadlock to which it must inevitably lead, in terms of the relation between Birkin and Ursula; but that exploration is really only one expression of a more deep-seated cultural crisis in Lawrence's life and work. Lawrence lived the breakdown of an old community, and knew intimately both its positive and negative effects: in recognising the strengths of that childhood society, he could also feel, in the fabric of his own experience, the points where its established boundaries needed to be transformed into horizons. At the highpoint of his literary achievement, in *The Rainbow*, he exploited that relation of conflict with his own culture to create one of the greatest novels of the century, discovering, with admirable certainty, the balance-point at which the old world he had known could be both inhabited from within and grasped, as a totality, from without. The tragedy of Lawrence—and it is, in this sense, a representative tragedy—was that, once the boundaries were crossed, there was nowhere else to go. There was no protected area within his own culture to which he could turn, for the evaluation of his own early experience which he could achieve in *Sons and Lovers* was inevitably a critique, not merely of his own class, but of the total class-structure of which that working environment was an expression. He turned, for a while, to alternative cultures beyond England, but always in the final knowledge that the problem of his own life could never be genuinely solved on that ground. The problem lay in his own society, and while Australia and New Mexico could provide momentary release and experiment, they could offer no enduring solution. A third area of traditional refuge, one gratefully or desperately embraced by a good many of Lawrence's contemporaries and successors, was also vigorously denied: the refuge of art itself. In the face of often intolerable pressures, Lawrence continued to stand out against the flight into aestheticism; in *Women in Love*, indeed, the falseness of that solution is firmly linked, in the relation of Loerke and Gudrun, with the falseness of expatriate escape. In all these ways, Lawrence refused bad faith and betrayal, at the price of an isolation which came finally, in my view, to affect the quality of his art. His importance to the theme of this study can be seen to lie in a simple fact: if few twentieth-century writers have paralleled Lawrence in his uncompromisingly total and revolutionary critique of English society, few also have achieved his inward understanding of its character. It is a paradox and a relationship significantly uncommon in the history of contemporary English literature.

CONCLUSION

I HAVE tried in this study to analyse certain aspects of what is, taken in its fullest range, a complex and intractable problem in the nature of the contemporary writer's relation to his work and culture. At the core of that problem has been a conflict which centres on the general paradox that literary art, like any achieved form of perception or cognition, demands a relationship of both operative distance from, and intricate inwardness with, its object. The argument of this book is that this general paradox has particular relevance in a society where, for reasons which I believe to be structural rather than accidental, the externality of the literal or metaphorical exile on the one hand, and a narrowly based empiricist naturalism on the other, have been common enough substitutes for genuine 'objectivity' and imaginative penetration.

It is important not to vulgarise the notions of exile and expatriation to some simple model of the 'outsider', with its banal imagery of a fixed ontological gap between isolated artist and inauthentic society. On the contrary, the felt experience of exile, as I have tried to show, takes a more subtle and diffused variety of forms. There is the complex ambiguity of a literal expatriate like Conrad, at work in *Under Western Eyes*: a range of attitudes towards the quality of native English culture, embodied in the habitual responses of that novel's narrator, in a dramatic encounter with alien modes of life. In my account of what I have termed the upper-class novel, in Woolf, Forster, Huxley and Waugh, that stance of literal exile undergoes a metaphorical transformation. The imagery of 'foreign parts'—India, Italy, Latin America—is still significantly present, but genuine exile now centres on a disorientated, isolatedly traditionalist, 'underground' or individualist subculture within English society itself. There are, evidently enough, notable differences in quality within this grouping:

differences, for example, between those 'free spirits' in Woolf, Forster, Huxley and early Waugh who can create a shared yet private space of real or fantastic liberation within the established social order, and, on the other hand, the tones which distinguish the later work of Waugh: the lonely voice, alternately sour and puzzled, angry and nostalgic, speaking from the margins of a society which is not only intolerably distasteful but now almost incomprehensible.

With Waugh in particular, the attachment to an older culture is strong enough to permit what becomes at times (and most obviously in *Brideshead Revisited*) a relatively uncomplicated opposition between 'tradition' and 'modernity'. Elsewhere in this grouping, the conflicts are more subtly discriminated, the explicit conservatism of *Brideshead* less assured. There is the inward conviction that one is, after all, the spiritually 'real' England (a conviction which links Forster's Schlegels with Waugh's aristocracy) and actual history mere aberration; less assertively, but still on essentially that model, there is the sense that one's own condition is unreal in a way which imbues a whole civilisation with illusion, and so deftly removes a constructive alternative. In both *Howard's End* and *Brideshead Revisited*, obviously different as those novels are, liberal or conservative values cannot be forgone, but neither can they be in any actual sense advanced or defended without a destructively opportunistic alliance with their enemies. The consequent feelings of ambivalence and rootlessness—the conflict, for instance, between an enduring commitment to the 'style' of one's social world coupled with an encroaching uneasiness about the substantial values which that style embodies—then lead directly to the imagery of exile and expatriation: to a half-desired, half-regretted spiritual self-distancing from a country which is still in some respects one's proprietary birthright, but which is temporarily or permanently occupied by aliens.

For the upper or upper middle class, those aliens inhabit the grey suburban world glimpsed in *Vile Bodies* from an aeroplane: the world of lower middle-class decencies and conventions to which George Orwell gave hesitant and self-doubting allegiance. It is, obviously enough, a world very different in texture and feeling from Waugh's: yet there can be little doubt, as one traces the recurrent forms of anxiety and alienation across the class-frontier, that they belong to substantially the same society. The lower middle-class world's defence against both the pieties and absurdities of 'high' culture and society is, at root, negative: an abrasive yet over-emphatic assertion of a lived 'reality' which is at once self-righteously flaunted and covertly detested. The flagrant anti-intellectualism of the world of Waugh, or the more subtle mimicry of responsible intellect of Huxley, are familiar targets of its criticism; yet its own habitual reflexes, rooted as they are in a tradition of withered empiricism hallowed as 'tough' and 'shrewd', merely confirm that abnegation of critical intellect at a different social level. To move from early Waugh to later Orwell is to pass from a condition in which deep-seated unease and neurosis is unable to achieve any formulation beyond a sporadic shaft of redundantly 'metaphysical' insight, to a world where structural criticism of the society is at once possible and dangerous. It is critical intelligence which lends the lower middle-class protagonist his imaginative edge over the surrounding 'masses'; it is that same intelligence which threatens to lead him into a self-betraying identity with the privileged unrealities of 'theory'. Again and again, Orwell's characters fall back by conscious choice from the brink of a total judgement to the raw stuff of pragmatic emotional impulse—an impulse which criticises and rejects, but which knows itself, in a cynical wisdom, to be subjective, unreliable and therefore, as a motive for the dangerous complexities of action, safely irrelevant.

The process of grasping any culture as a whole, of discerning its essential forms and directions, is always, needless to say, an acutely difficult task; but that difficulty seems significantly exacerbated in modern English society. It has been part of the purpose of this study to suggest, from certain partial and selected angles, why this might be so. The English novel of the eighteenth and nineteenth centuries, from Defoe to Dickens, was the product of a confident and expanding middle class whose characteristic concerns, in the problems of value, consciousness, relationship and identity, sufficiently coincided with the definitive problems and directions of the society as a whole to allow it 'representative' status. It is that status which can be seen in the process of collapse towards the end of the nineteenth century, as the major realist tradition is transmuted into new forms. On the one hand, the intensifying problems of value, relationship and identity, raised by a society in prolonged crisis, broke beyond the traditional forms of literary realism within which they had been previously confined. From this movement emerged a kind of novel forced back on to crucial questions of private consciousness and individual value in a society whose actual character came to seem increasingly elusive and remote. A form of novel embodying many of the ideal values, definitions and aspirations of a traditional middle class, often in its best liberal or conservative modes, is driven increasingly to confront, and to withdraw from, the harsh actualities of the society which that same class has largely created. It is from this source, and from other sources related to it, that the characteristic feelings of guilt, cynicism, nostalgia, impotent idealism and fantasy can then be seen to flow. On the other hand, there emerged from the erosion of the realist tradition a trenchant but static naturalism which again, in its response to the apparently shapeless insistence of common experience, broke beyond the habitual forms of realism. Neither of these forms could be 'representative' in the traditional sense: between them, the modern novel was polarised into a remote and eclectic idealism, and a deeply fragmented empiricism.

I have argued that the vacuum created by this polarisation was filled in one way by the recourse to myth. In the internally coherent and autonomous realm of mythology, that total understanding which the shape of English culture actively forestalled was achieved by a displacement of attention outside the confines of English, or indeed of any particular historical society. I have tried to demonstrate the qualities of that mode, especially in relation to Eliot, as a way of defining more closely the nature of such total understanding in modern literature, and its difference from imposed or monolithic ways of seeing. It is the conflict between those two kinds of totality—the one alertly responsive to the movement of specific life within a sense of the whole, the other essentially inert and extrinsic— which occurs in an acute form within the work of D. H. Lawrence. It is in Eliot, Yeats and Lawrence—all of them, in different ways, strangers in part to the system I have described —that the materials of a directly personal response to the quality of a whole society can be worked and extended into confidently public and representative terms.

INDEX